property of: (

W9-BBN-410

698-4013

UNJUST JUSTICE

Crosscurrents

ISI Books' Crosscurrents series makes available in English, usually for the first time, new translations of both classic and contemporary works by authors working within, or with crucial importance for, the conservative, religious, and humanist intellectual traditions.

TITLES IN SERIES

Equality by Default, by Philippe Bénéton, trans. by Ralph C. Hancock
A Century of Horrors, by Alain Besançon, trans. by Ralph C. Hancock and Nathaniel Hancock
Critics of the Enlightenment, ed. and trans. by Christopher O. Blum
Icarus Fallen, by Chantal Delsol, trans. by Robin Dick
The Unlearned Lessons of the Twentieth Century, by Chantal Delsol, trans. by Robin Dick
Democracy wihout Nations? by Pierre Manent, trans. by Paul Seaton
Tradition: Concept and Claim, by Josef Pieper, trans. by E. Christian Kopff

UNJUST JUSTICE

AGAINST THE TYRANNY OF INTERNATIONAL LAW

Chantal Delsol

TRANSLATED WITH AN INTRODUCTION BY

Paul Seaton

ISI BOOKS

Wilmington, Delaware

Delsol, Chantal, 1947–

[Grande méprise. English]
Unjust justice : against the tyranny of international law / Chantal Delsol ; translated with an introduction by Paul Seaton.—1st English ed. —Wilmington, Del. : ISI Books, c2008.

p. ; cm.
(Crosscurrents)

ISBN: 978-1-933859-07-1
Originally published in French as: La grande méprise : justice internationale, gouvernement mondial, guerre juste : essai (Paris : Table ronde, 2004).

1. Law and ethics. 2. Criminal justice, Administration of--Philosophy. 3. International law—Philosophy. I. Seaton, Paul, 1954–II. Title. III. Title: Grande méprise. IV. Series: Crosscurrents (Wilmington, Del.)

KZ1256 .D4513 2008 2007942688
341.1/12—dc22 0807

Originally published in France in 2004 as *Le Grande Méprise*

English translation published in the United States by:
ISI Books
Intercollegiate Studies Institute
Post Office Box 4431
Wilmington, DE 19807-0431
www.isibooks.org

Manufactured in the United States of America

CONTENTS

TRANSLATOR'S PREFACE

WITH *UNJUST JUSTICE: AGAINST THE TYRANNY OF INTERNATIONAL LAW*, the contemporary French political philosopher Chantal Delsol completes a trilogy of studies devoted to an analysis of "the spirit of late modernity." *Icarus Fallen* and *The Unlearned Lessons of the Twentieth Century* looked at post–Cold War Europe and sought to describe and analyze the dominant "spirit of the times." It is a rebuffed, but not particularly repentant, spirit, that of "Icarus" or "modern man." The modern spirit is deeply "impatient with limits"; it is also steadfastly "progressive," whether in a more gentle liberal-progressive manner or in a brutal totalitarian mode. Both approaches assume the perfectibility of man and the conquerability, so to speak, of nature. They attempt to implement, with modern ideologies and instruments, the age-old Promethean aspiration.

With the collapse of communism and the "return" of social and human problems that Progress was supposed to have relegated to History's dustbin, contemporary modern man—Icarus Fallen—is confounded, dazed and confused. The old idols have been toppled, having shown themselves to possess feet of clay. Where to look for one's bearings? What is there to look forward—if not "up"—to? Modern man has returned to what Delsol calls "the labyrinth of mediocrity"—the essential constituents and conundra of the human condition—and he does not know how to orient himself.

Nevertheless, he is quite sure how to organize the international scene. He has drawn specific lessons from the experience of Nazi totalitarianism, especially from the Holocaust (not from communism, though, because communism was one of his erstwhile acceptable options). He is very much a proponent of "international law" and of a distinctive form of justice: "international justice." These are the dictates of modern man's newest form of democratic humanitarianism. The essentials of contemporary democratic morality—human rights, respect for difference, the lessons drawn from the Holocaust—must become the touchstones of a global legal and judicial order. Originating and taking root in Europe, this understanding of international law and justice presents itself as a model for the rest of humanity. In this way, as the first instantiation and harbinger of a brighter future for all humanity, Europe can do penance for its missionary, colonial, and imperial past.

Writing in the midst of this dominant ideology, Delsol is quite countercultural (hence the appropriateness of her inclusion in a series titled "Crosscurrents"). Her resistance, though, is with graceful pen, cogent reasoning, and rhetorical deftness. She argues that this humanitarian vision and project is deeply flawed in terms of its premises, its means, and its aim. Her critique combines several threads.

First, she contrasts contemporary progressive thinking—for example, that of Jürgen Habermas—with earlier European proponents of human liberty, progress, and the rule of law, the "moderate Enlightenment thinkers" Montesquieu and Kant. The differences between the two sets of thinkers are revealing. Montesquieu was aware of the tyrannical potentials in Enlightenment thought itself, and he was a much sturdier defender of human diversity and a better practitioner of genuine cultural understanding than the proponents of international law typically can allow themselves to be. As for Kant, he more rigorously distinguished the moral order from the legal order than they; he did so in order to respect both human liberty and the nature of morality itself. Contemporary legal moralism conflates and distorts both. Here, Delsol's contrasts are decidedly invidious and, I confess, delightful to consider.

It is a further wicked pleasure to see Delsol so aptly liken the spirit of contemporary legal moralism to the Inquisition, to the misplaced "dogmatism" of a church that Enlightenment thought originally sought to replace. Moderate Enlightenment's original spirit of deep respect for individual conscience and of patient skepticism towards all positions, *including towards one's own convictions and certainties,* is not replicated by a contemporary moralistic and legalistic clerisy. As she makes quite clear, not all dogmatisms are religious, especially in a resolutely secular age.

Delsol herself is not simply a woman of the moderate Enlightenment, however. As a political philosopher, she has her own criteria of judgment. These include the core values of human liberty, cultural and even ontological diversity, and the adventure (and risks) of "political decision." In their light she deflates much progressive glibness, unmasks its hypocrisies, and exposes the logic of its necessarily tyrannical prosecution and consequences. In so doing, she both renders the values and virtues of her own position more attractive—the real thing is more solid and precious than ersatz simulacra—and she lays out more honestly and helpfully the requirements their advance entails. An alternative, if plodding, subtitle for this book might read: "an artful defense of the human values of liberty, political deliberation, and genuine respect for diversity." Happily, Delsol's prose itself is never clunky.

As a specifically *political* philosopher, Delsol is particularly sensitive to the requirements of genuine political community and of effective political action (including the search for and realization of justice itself). As a philosopher *tout court,* she provocatively situates her assessment of the contemporary scene within a broader context. She has definite anthropological views regarding the nature of the human race and of the human person, as well as a general understanding of "culture" as a humanizing response to the enigmas and "tragic" features of man's being-in-the world. To this general concept of culture she adds an illuminating perspective on one culture in particular: the West. Contemporary Western men and women receive from her the homage of the philosopher's full attention: she tries to take their full measure in all three dimensions of their being—anthropological, civilizational, and historical (that is, in their peculiar status as late moderns). Having incisively critiqued one of their most cherished contemporary illusions, she intellectually liberates them, so that they may continue the human adventure with an improved *connaissance de cause humaine.*

I WOULD LIKE to acknowledge and thank two individuals and an institution. Heartfelt thanks to Chantal Delsol, intrepid spirit and warm personality, and to Jeremy Beer, editor in chief at ISI Books, connoisseur of literary merit and similar spirit. Neither is among Burke's "good men who do nothing." And thanks to ISI Books for its estimable contribution to contemporary culture. May the seeds it sows continue to bear fruit.

A final note on the text: all footnotes are mine, while the author's own notes are indicated by numerals and are included in the Notes section that begins on page 135.

Paul Seaton
Baltimore, Maryland
April 2008

AUTHOR'S NOTE

THIS SHORT BOOK on the new version of international law and justice develops several themes that I have already sketched in two previous books, *Icarus Fallen* and *The Unlearned Lessons of the Twentieth Century.* This further treatment thus constitutes the continuation and the culmination of a series of works devoted to the spirit of late modernity. The current European passion for international law and justice to my mind represents a significant example of the contemporary loss of contact with reality as well as its demiurgic impulse. Besides what it owes to the ideologies of the twentieth century, this loss of contact with reality is one of the consequences of an epoch in which comfort and ease have taken away almost all sense of the tragic in life. It is therefore very likely that we are merely transitional figures bound to disappear along with the epoch when true history once again reappears. Nonetheless I want to bring to light some characteristic traits of the error-filled time we are living through. The hoped-for unity of humanity and the type of justice sought are not the objects of *conquest,* which is what we want to make people believe, in large part through our strident discourses, but of an always imperfectly realized *quest,* a search which alone gives meaning to history.

The universal state is not simply a goal prescribed by reason, which we believe that an adequate effort will allow us to attain in a systematic manner. If it were merely that, if it were only postulated by logic and morality, our future would be severely compromised. Therefore we hold it is also something that is already underway. The shadow that it casts ahead of itself obscures all the old images, undermines all the familiar justifications, those above all concerning the state and its exigencies. That is why the wars of the historical states become so suspect, their borders so doubtful. The future that is coming to sight breaks with their norms; it announces itself by means of other images and other principles, and also by a new form of law.

—E. JÜNGER
THE UNIVERSAL STATE

INTRODUCTION

MORALITY PLACED ABOVE ANY RELIGIOUS OR SECULAR FAITH

ONE DAY GOD required Abraham to sacrifice to him his son, Isaac. By this awful command God indicated that Abraham must agree to obey him even if it meant contravening the moral law. Inscribed in the heart of conscience, the moral law is valid for the entire community; it imposes itself as a limit and norm that structures the living-together of the community. Abraham was and remained bewildered before this paradoxical command. How could God oppose himself to the moral law? In this case, to which of the two authorities should he submit? Nonetheless, Abraham obeyed: he loved God with a magnificent love, a love that justifies all sacrifices.

The question of the suspension of the ethical for the sake of faith was, of course, famously meditated upon by Kierkegaard in his great book *Fear and Trembling.* Morality refers to a *common* law, while the individual who finds himself alone before the Absolute lives in a *singular* relationship. The sacrifice that God demanded of Abraham cast him into anguish, fear and trembling, because in the eyes of the ethical man God demanded a murder and, even worse, an infanticide.

We know that God eventually took the knife from the hands of the horror-stricken but obedient father. From this we must conclude that God cannot oppose himself to morality. What remains troubling, though, is that he went so far—almost to the bitter end—to impose this test on Abraham.

Today the death of the gods has relegated all authority to the sphere of immanence. In the twentieth century the governments of certain regimes required their subjects to abandon common morality. The story of Abraham was repeated by the adherents of communism and National Socialism. They were required to forget the commands of their moral conscience, at least for a time (they were told), in order to prove their faith in ideology, an ideology embodied in the leaders who gave these orders. We know that the enormity of the paradox did not escape these secular believers, because it sometimes was necessary to get them drunk or otherwise intoxicated before sending them out to do their awful deeds.

Some readers will be angry at me for comparing the God of Abraham to the totalitarian despots of the twentieth century. Please note, however, that I am not comparing persons but *situations*—at least in their initial stages, because our contemporary despots did not send an angel to stay the hands of their subjects at the last moment. In both cases we find a situation where the supreme authority contradicts morality in the name of a faith. The murderous character of the twentieth century emerged from this contest between faith and morality, with faith winning out all too often.

This is why we who bear the burden of these traumatizing experiences prefer the just man, the one who above all respects the moral principles dictated by conscience, to the saint who places obedience to an arbitrary authority ahead of those principles. To be candid, because of this preference the religious person seems suspect to us.

The contemporary resolve to establish institutions of international justice comes from a desire to make ethics or morality everywhere supreme over obedience to a leader or to a system. It represents a promise that never again will morality be supplanted by faith. We must punish those individuals who believe that they are permitted to violate commonly held morality under the pretext that it has been commanded by an authoritative leader, by an ideology, or by the importance of some historical task.

Therefore, a form of international criminal justice has begun to emerge since the end of the Cold War. It necessarily entails a world government. The two are bound together; the one implies the other. However, at this point in time—fifteen years after the establishment of the International Criminal Court for the former Yugoslavia (1993) and six years after the ratification of the convention providing for the creation of a permanent International Criminal Court (2002)—it is clear that we live in an intermediate, and therefore unstable and uncomfortable, situation. Why? Today's international criminal justice only punishes certain criminals, those who can be apprehended because they belong to countries that find themselves in a weak and dependent position. Even if China and Russia were to ratify the treaty establishing the International Criminal Court, would the court be able to judge Chinese authorities for what they have done to Tibet? Or put Putin in the dock for crimes committed in Chechnya? Of course not.

For this reason, for the time being international criminal justice is not so much a kind of justice but a sort of private vengeance of the kind that one would find in the state of nature before the emergence of law. In the state of nature I punish my neighbor for his crime because I saw him do it or because I suffered from his actions; I do so above all because I *can* capture and control him.

To be sure, the international justice that we have instituted defines the crimes subject to its jurisdiction (crimes against humanity, genocide, war crimes), but it does not prosecute all those who might be charged. Far from it. It only prosecutes those whose relatively unfortunate diplomatic circumstances allow them to be apprehended, and those whose deeds provoke the most indignation among the Western public. This is not at all how justice worthy of the name should work. It should be applicable to all or to none, and it should operate in a well-defined territory without any exceptions. One quite rightly would criticize the scandal of a purportedly French justice that judged criminals of Bretagne but refused to prosecute those of Midi-Pyrénées because powerful political figures were able to protect them by threatening reprisals!

To render justice does not consist in judging and punishing a few malefactors whose existence inconveniences and disturbs our moral conscience, while letting alone those whom we find excusable because their intentions were good (former Communists for example) or those where the effort to apprehend them would be futile. Justice does not have "making examples" as its vocation. To render justice is to reaffirm and strengthen a common world by defining limits and norms common to all; it is to bring peace to a society in which all without exception are subject to law. With self-proclaimed "international" or "global" justice it must apply to all the individuals on the planet or it will miss its aim.

That is why the present situation must appear as temporary and provisional, as a sort of intermediate historical period in which we have learned the necessity of punishing state criminals but without yet being able to establish true justice. It is, therefore, an unjust justice, because while it is purportedly established for the entire planet it only applies to a few. The only way to confer on international justice its true stature would be to establish a government that had the force of law over all the world.

A number of authors have recently underscored this obvious requirement of a government actually capable of effecting this specific form of justice. For example, Tzvetan Todorov: "The promotion of universal justice implies the construction of a universal state. In order to effectively promote justice one needs police forces who apprehend criminals and gather witnesses; if justice is to be universal, police will have to be as well. Police, in their turn, have to be subject to the orders of a government—and this also tends toward unity and universality."[1] Jürgen Habermas: "We find ourselves in a dilemma, constrained to act as if an international law already existed, while that is exactly what must be advanced."[2] Pierre Hassner: "As long as a world government does not exist we will remain in an in-between condition, in constant perplexity over what the United Nations and the states to whom it has delegated authority can and cannot do. . . . We are in an intermediate stage."[3] François Terré: "The absence of a universal state critically weakens with particular force, especially where justice is concerned, the first outlines of an international criminal order."[4]

International justice is not a form of pacifism. It does not rule out force or violence, but it wants them to unite legality and legitimacy. State violence can be legal without being legitimate. Wartime violence can be legitimate without being legal. We therefore have to transform the act of war into a police act conducted by a truly *moral* state. But there must be a state. Only a state can transform natural justice or law—in the name of which international law claims to speak—into positive law, i.e., norms backed by power.

The establishment of an ad hoc international tribunal to judge the crimes committed in the former Yugoslavia or those in Rwanda, and the creation of an International Criminal Court, represent the first steps toward a world government. Not in the sense that they make it possible, but in the sense that they make it necessary by having created an intermediate situation incapable of lasting very long, given the injustice that it itself commits.

But does universal justice exist? At what price can one establish it?

CHAPTER 1

GENEALOGY: FROM UNIVERSAL EMPIRE TO THE WORLD STATE

THE IDEA OF establishing a unified, universal political order capable of bringing peoples together under the reign of justice and thus putting an end to war emerged long ago with Alexander the Great and later Caracalla; it resurfaced at the time of Christian Europe. Both Dante's idea of a universal monarchy and the reality of the Germanic Holy Roman empire corresponded to Christendom's desire to embody its spiritual universality in a political form. In the sixteenth and seventeenth centuries the empire, and Christendom as a whole, had to renounce their claims to universality because of the rise of national states and the emergence of the modern concept of sovereignty. The church retreated into spiritual universality, while the idea of political universality disappeared. The universal forms desired first by the ancients and then by Christians were very different from what appeared in modern times during the French Revolution. The difference consisted in two things.

Among the ancients the universal empire did not embrace the entirety of the planet, but only that portion occupied by the Greeks and later by the Romans. In their eyes it was vast, but it was quite small compared to the entire world, which was incompletely known by them. They considered the outsiders they knew to be barbarians. But the existence of these countless vaguely known peoples located beyond the limits of the civilized world relativized the idea of the universal and allowed for a distinction between *us* and *them*. The ancient empire did not encompass the globe. It left diversity in place. Because it was not monopolistic, because an outside perspective could judge it, it hardly resembled the world government proposed by moderns. As long as Tacitus could write a *Germania*,* there was no cosmopolis.

Among the Christians, on the other hand, the universality was truly global. It ideally included all peoples, even the most barbarous, because all are called to enter into the kingdom of God. However, Christians distinguished that kingdom from worldly ones. The goal was neither to establish worldwide laws nor a single state but to spiritually convince peoples and cultures, which would otherwise retain their differences.

Until the eighteenth century, therefore, the idea of a thoroughly universal unity was limited on one hand by the relative modesty of the actual imperial territory and the great extent of the surrounding world, and on the other by the restriction of its rule to spiritual ends by the Christian community.

With the French Revolution, we see the two ideas combined for the first time. What emerged was the notion of a world government deployed throughout the entire earth with all the prerogatives of what Christians called "temporal government."

The French revolutionaries demanded the abolition of borders and their replacement by a universal republic: "The division of the human race into different peoples is like feudal anarchy . . . and two sovereigns on the earth are as absurd as two gods in heaven"[1] wrote Anacharsis Cloots, who also spoke of his "aversion to the fragmentation of the world."[2] As we will see, the denial of diversity is rooted in the absolute certainty that only one right way of life exists.

---

* Gaius Cornelius Tacitus (c. 56–c. 117), Roman senator and historian; his *Germania* (ca. 98) was an ethnographic work on the diverse Germanic peoples or tribes outside the Roman empire.

Marxists looked forward to the first truly universal state, one that would cover the entire globe. The purpose of its unity was the realization of homogeneity. The universal state encompassing the entire world was to be "socially homogenous," that is, without classes.[3] Established in London in 1864, the First International called itself the International *Workingmen's* Association. And despite events—especially wars—to the contrary (because they continued to place issues in the context of outdated nationalisms), the constant effort of the various Internationals until the 1960s was to abolish borders. When national exigencies were imposed upon socialism, Trotskyite movements took up the torch of internationalism. The dream of a worldwide proletarian revolution leading to a world government and classless society still appears in French neo-Trotskyite literature.

Current opponents of globalization rebel against the domination of a single vision of the world. That vision, as is well known, is that of economic and political liberalism, the "democracy of the market," as it is sometimes called. It is not imposed by force or even by the threat of force, but rather constantly develops on its own and is currently uncontested, since no real alternative has presented itself since the fall of the Berlin Wall. The few remaining recalcitrant countries (such as Cuba and North Korea) will eventually have to go along, because their political-economic systems lead only to ruin.

At the beginning, then, globalization was a Communist idea. Today, it finally seems to be coming to fruition by means of liberalism. Put another way, history's real irony is that globalization is being realized by the opponents of those who initially proposed it.

Therefore, the Western groups that rebel and rail against globalization, whether at Genoa or elsewhere, only reveal half of their thought to the public. They really do not oppose globalization as such, but *liberal* globalization. And what they really wish to defend is not diversity or pluralism in the face of a single form of thought that is being imposed universally. Rather, they want to direct themselves the process of homogenization—they want it to occur under their banner.

This is a form of deception, because the unsuspecting person who opens his newspaper in the morning believes it when he reads that the opponents of globalization are defending his "right to difference," while in truth they are only resisting the winners' version of globalization.

The ideology defended by antiglobalists is really a new globalist ideology erected on the ruins of "real socialism," and it is still animated by a hatred of triumphant liberalism. The moralizing, pontificating nongovernmental organizations (NGOs) present at the 2001 Durbin conference against racism, etc., provided a striking illustration. Called "transnational progressivism,"[4] or "neoprogressivism,"[5] this current of antiglobalism draws from the Marxism of Gramsci and interprets the world according to an eternal conflict between oppressors and oppressed. It presents itself as the only alternative to liberal globalization. But it echoes the latter's dogmatic and monopolistic certitude. It envisages the elimination of state sovereignties and, when it does not simply abolish the term "citizen," it speaks of the "transnational citizen" or "global citizen." The latter is like the ancient stoic notion of the "citizen of the world," except this time he is stripped of all particular identities or affiliations and bears only a global identity.

However, the antiglobalists find themselves stymied, incapable of any forward movement, by the stark contrast between their ideal society and today's society. Their ideal irresistibly recalls the Communist episode that people today have no desire to revisit. Thus, they claim to be "anti"-globalists rather than "alternative" globalists. They have to stop short at the stage of negation or denial, which makes them look like the nihilists of old. It will not be under their auspices that a new universalism will come to be, because what they have to propose in this vein is so suspect.

The new universalism shows up rather in the speech of those partisans of democracy who are adept at talking about human rights. This discourse is partly now so persuasive because it was uttered by the true heroes of earlier times: the dissidents. They understood the monstrosity of totalitarianism and devoted themselves single-mindedly to the work of recognizing human dignity. A few decades ago it was the Marxists who were considered paragons of generosity and humanity. Today the side of the angels is taken—the camp of the good is represented—by the democratic defenders of human rights.

The world government now being sought therefore has changed its nature along with the transformation of its proponents. It is no longer thought of as the result or expression of real universal equality, nor as a statist machine designed to produce a new humanity. Rather, it is presented as a means of establishing justice at the level of the entire globe, aimed especially against *states* that oppress their peoples. Ever since Garry Davis, the first postwar "citizen of the world," world government has seemed to be the sole effective way of responding to the horrors of wars between nations and of injustices within them.[6]

During the 1950s the motivation for world government was the need for peace, in the context of the nuclear threat, among those nations torn apart by the two world wars.[7] Today local, internal wars between historical rivals have resurfaced, which is probably why world government is called for in the name of justice rather than peace. While it may appear less utopian, this new ambition nonetheless raises disturbing questions, which this book addresses. Our contemporaries no longer seek a "*socially* homogenous universal state," as Alexandre Kojève put it during the time of communism, but rather a *morally* homogenous universal state. It is natural that this rather vague ambient idea of a world government should be put at the service of the dominant value of the times. Today, for very understandable historical reasons, morality is more important to us than the equality of social classes. We have learned that the equalization of classes does not perfect but rather destroys societies.

The goal of the contemporary defender of human rights is to establish the worldwide reign of justice by means of global tribunals, without any possibility of appeal. In this way, the new internationalism organizes itself under the banner of the judge, not the commissioner.

Some may say that world government is an attractive but unreal utopia, of the sort which resurfaces on a regular basis. A few idealists and intellectuals detached from concrete life make it their mantra, while the world moves on without them. Why should we concern ourselves with them, or it? Well, because today a concrete step has been taken towards its realization: the creation of courts of international criminal justice. In general, the debates between its partisans—various NGOs, most European countries—and its detractors—those who have not ratified the treaty establishing the International Criminal Court, including the United States (and in fact all the most populous and powerful countries in the world)—are conducted in terms of a debate between moral idealism and *Realpolitik*. This debate, however, seems to me to miss the essential point. My aim here is not to demonstrate the unrealistic character of world government, its concrete impossibility—in short, its utopian character. On the contrary, while maintaining that it is possible because it *has begun* to be realized via institutions of international criminal justice, I want to show its injurious, even disastrous character. Put another way, it is the legitimacy and desirability of international criminal justice and of world government that interest me, not their ability or inability to be established in the real world. Everything is possible, and history can give rise to anything. The real question to ask is, what is desirable?

In point of fact the arguments by which the demand for international justice has been established have their grounds and are coherent. The political societies that exist today in the context of globalization no longer are self-sufficient; they cannot pretend to autarchy or to yesterday's sovereignty. The more that commercial and other exchanges develop, the more that interdependence makes itself felt, the more that the need for a common good which is global and not merely national becomes clear. This need corresponds to a very human exigency: the aspiration toward the universal, the desire to leave the narrow confines of the city—one's particular political community—and to share values, ideas, and goods with all of humanity. Moreover, the more that remorse for the disasters of the twentieth century grows—and this remorse cannot fail to grow as the veil over the Communist past is withdrawn—the more the desire to stop the great and petty tyrants of the earth will grow. What more noble aim can there be than to battle and defeat Evil wherever it may be found on earth? Why, therefore, should one oppose this beautiful and generous idea, that of cosmopolitan justice? It should be opposed because it undermines politics and, more generally, human diversity, both of which must be preserved. In defending politics and diversity, though, must we therefore deny the very idea of world justice? Not really. We must redefine it, though, in terms of other reference points than those to which the last two centuries have accustomed us.

CHAPTER 2

COSMOPOLITANISM AND UTOPIA: THE RELEVANCE OF THE LATER KANT

IN A WORK published in 1784 titled *The Idea of a Universal History from a Cosmopolitan Point of View*, Kant described the progress of humanity as the development of the human faculties during the long process of historical development. The short life of a single human does not leave him the time necessary to develop all his endowments, but through the accumulation of experience the human *race* can arrive at the ever more complete development to which the individual aspires. This idea is characteristic of an epoch that had not yet seen the barbarisms of the twentieth century, crimes which called into question the hope for human perfection, much less in perfectibility. It should not be consigned to the museum of antiquities, however. On the contrary, despite all our deceptions and disappointments (perhaps because of them), at the beginning of the twenty-first century we have never been closer to realizing what Kant regarded as "the supreme aim of nature: a universal cosmopolitan state."[1] In writing this, Kant put his finger on the most ardent hope of humanity, as well as the greatest difficulty in realizing it. (To be sure, humanity can also refuse to hope for anything and content itself with meaningless chaos and a purposeless history). This hope is "the establishment of a civil society which administers law universally."[2] We find ourselves at the beginning stage of the realization of this project.

In order to realize this work of reason, we will have to create a world state—*Weltstaat*. The world state capable of assuring justice between and among the many states, which until then will conduct themselves like individuals in the state of nature, will play the same role that a particular state plays vis-à-vis private vendettas. In the same way that it was earlier possible to end the state of nature between men and groups of men only by means of states, in the same way the state of nature, or the war of all against all found among states, will be brought to an end by the world state.

Kant invoked this world state in works published during the 1780s: in 1784 in *The Idea of a Universal History*,[3] and in 1786, although in a rather imprecise way, in *Conjectures on the Beginnings of Human History*. But beginning with the 1790s his thinking changed. In the third part of *Theory and Practice* (1793), which is devoted to the *jus gentium*, the law of nations, the cosmopolitan constitution capable of bringing universal peace becomes more dangerous than war itself, because it "brings with it the most frightening despotism."[4] The universal state still represents the historical hope of a humanity endlessly seeking perfection, but it has a changed nature. It henceforth is a question of "a state, to be sure, but one which is not a cosmopolitan community subject to a leader, it is a *federated* state subject to a *law of nations* to which all the member-states have agreed."[5]

This change in perspective finds its completion in a text of 1795, *Project of a Universal Peace*. In it Kant clearly replaces the project, or hope, for a world state with the project or hope for a federation of free states that together would be capable of promoting justice and peace in the world.

The federation of free states is described as "a negative replacement,"[6] a sort of substitute, for the world state. All the supposed capacity or ability of this federation to promote perpetual peace is based on the following postulate: republican societies are peaceful because in them it is the *people* who decide on peace and war, and if kings prefer war, peoples prefer peace. (This peace, however, is not guaranteed because one cannot eradicate human wickedness, only domesticate it under laws.) The federation of free states therefore is a kernel or core of republican states, which gradually can convince the rest of the planet to imitate and join them.

Kant's movement from the first period to the second is equivalent to a break or rupture. He moves from the idea of a world state regulating all peoples to "a contract of free and permanent association"[7] animating a federation. The reason informing this change is important for us today.

One might think that Kant abandoned the idea of a world state in order to escape the charge of utopianism. We know how sensitive he was to this charge, and we also know the mockery directed during this time toward the work of l'abbé de Saint-Pierre, a work that Kant knew well. At the end of the eighteenth century utopias were everywhere. Kant did not want to be included in the company of those amiable narrators of impossible perfection. However, it was not this consideration that changed his mind about world government. Rather, it was the difficulties the realization of the idea would present. It was as if Kant saw that this "utopia" was at once feasible and terrifying. In this perception, he preceded Berdiaev, who said (according to Orwell's formulation): "Utopias appear to be much more feasible than was believed before. We find ourselves before a new and troubling question: How to avoid their actual realization? . . . [P]erhaps a new century begins in which intellectuals and the educated class will dream of the means of avoiding utopias and of returning to a nonutopian society that is less *perfect* and more *free*." Kant saw that the perpetual peace of world government had to be purchased at the price of liberty, and he decided in favor of liberty: "A federation of states having as its sole aim the avoidance of war is the only lawful state compatible with the liberty of all of them."[8]

We find ourselves today at a moment when both of Kant's projects, whether of the first period or the second, can be realized. Hence the relevance of his thought.

And yet Kant's concluding reflections, to the effect that we must do without a world government in order to avoid the reign of the "peace of the cemetery," terribly limit our present hopes. If Kant is right, the world state is possible but not desirable—we should rather say, it is horrifying—and if we can attempt to limit conflicts and wars we cannot eradicate them. This is why Jürgen Habermas in 1996 published an interpretation of the Kantian idea in light of the contemporary world.[9] His goal was to demonstrate that Kant's reservations vis-à-vis the world state depended upon the circumstances of his day rather than on any anthropological reason, any reason pertaining to human nature.

According to Habermas, two undeniable contemporary realities call into question Kant's conclusions. First of all, Kant lived at the time of state sovereignty as articulated by Bodin,* and he could not admit—nor could his contemporaries—what we call the right of intervention. Today, sovereignty in this sense has practically disappeared, and the political agents whose liberty Kant wanted to preserve have already lost it. The world has already become an "involuntary community."[10] In addition, Kant's time was not yet familiar with world wars and wars of annihilation: today, these criminal wars "call war itself into question as a crime."[11]

According to Habermas, it is therefore time to oblige states to respect human rights, and in order to do that we must sketch the project of a "cosmopolitan democracy," one with a world parliament and endowed with a permanent International Court of Justice. This organization would have at its disposal an armed force that would allow it "to exercise police functions" and thus replace war with police action.[12]

Fearing that he might be accused of wanting to establish a *moral* world order, of advocating a sort of human-rights fundamentalism, Habermas tries to show that the above-mentioned institutions are not

* Jean Bodin (1529–96), French jurist and political philosopher. The first theoretician of modern state sovereignty. He laid out his thoughts in his most famous work, *Six Books on the Republic* (1576).

of a moral nature—even if "their foundation rests exclusively on the moral point of view"[13]—but rather are juridical or legal, or at least can become legal with the establishment of a cosmopolitan state. The status of human rights is at issue here, and we will discuss it later.

I do not think that we can simply analyze Kant's arguments through the prism of "his time." It seems to me that these arguments transcend their circumstances, remain pertinent today, and likely will be pertinent tomorrow. They are based less on a historical situation than on a type of philosophical reflection concerning man. In fact it is probably distrust of such philosophical reflection that prompts people to read Kant's arguments contextually.

The fact that we have entered into a post-Bodinan or post-Westphalian era, leaving behind sovereignty in the strict or absolute sense of the term, can only help us understand why we have much less difficulty than our predecessors in understanding and agreeing to a right and duty of intervention. This, however, is something of a return to the concept of just war, which was well established in the pre-Bodinan period.

Furthermore, the question of world government is not properly posed at a simply historical level. We can agree that state sovereignty represents a temporary, a historically conditioned, type of political authority, one relative to an epoch. The question of the establishment of a world government, however, is not properly engaged by the question, can we do without *state* sovereignty? We have to ask more broadly: Can we do without any and all forms of particular *political* authority? The erosion of state sovereignty today gives rise to its replacement by all sorts of intermediate or different authorities, which, because they pertain to the organization of societies as wholes and refer to the public good, can be called "political."

Kant, moreover, does not exactly insist on the *sovereignty* of states but on the *liberty* of political authorities. In the fifth paragraph of his *Project of a Universal Peace,* where he announces the principle of noninterference or nonintervention, Kant does not argue for the omnipotence or autarchy of the sovereign state. Why, he asks, would we interject ourselves by force in the affairs of another state? Would it be because of the scandal that the actions of that state causes us? This reason rings true to our contemporary ears. It is the scandal that leads us to intervention. But Kant responds differently: "The bad example that a free person gives to another does not constitute an assault on the latter."

In other words, intervention between states is not an act of legitimate defense and therefore is not justified. The *freedom* of states insofar as they are *moral persons* who are masters of their own positive law but not subject to a superior positive law makes any intervening action of a foreign power illegitimate. The term "scandal" conveys very well that the intervention in this case is provoked by *moral* indignation. But what is essential to morality is freedom. And one cannot constrain a free agent because of moral reasons; one can only constrain him in accordance with legal norms, which do not exist between states.

One of the questions posed by the project of world government, therefore, is to know not if state sovereignty has disappeared but if *political* institutions still ought to exist as moral persons—i.e., as free and responsible for their acts even if these actions appear to others as scandalous.

The second argument is different. It says that the conflicts of the twentieth century became total wars in the sense of wars of extermination (thus suggesting that in the past there were not any wars of extermination, which is a debatable claim). Does the prevention of wars that are now in themselves considered crimes justify the creation of a world state? The affirmative answer takes on a very different meaning when one notices that the advocates of the right of intervention and of world government propose a different goal than did Kant. Kant sought peace. Today the ultimate goal is not peace but justice by means of the defense of human rights, even if this defense requires the violence of war. In order to render Habermas's argument coherent, therefore, one would need to distinguish in a quite objective way criminal wars from just wars, something that no one is attempting to do.

The Kantian idea of progress, at least in the aspect that concerns us, is not based on a vague utopian dream. Kant rightly remarks that men always judge peace preferable to war, justice to injustice, and law to violence. Even if men wage war, commit injustice, and perpetrate violence, this homage that vice pays to virtue naturally contains and conveys hope. Who would deny that the search for perpetual peace is "a duty of practical reason,"[14] "a task that, gradually accomplished, will bring reason to an end which is its own"?[15] Who denies that as human beings we have the vocation of trying to realize justice with all of our strength? But would a world government bring about the reign of justice?

CHAPTER 3

THE HOLOCAUST AS TOUCHSTONE AND CRITERION OF CRIMES AGAINST HUMAN RIGHTS

FOR TWO CENTURIES European thought lived in the relativism inaugurated by the philosophies of suspicion (Marx, Darwin, Nietzsche). Once natural law was denied only positive law counted. The sacralization of the nation added to this conviction. With the disappearance of transcendence and the consequent disappearance of absolute norms anchored in a stable anthropology (which also was jettisoned), the law of the state no longer found itself before any alternative superior to it and able to call it into question. State crimes could therefore occur without principled objection: in the absence of natural right or natural law the leader—Stalin, Hitler, Mao, etc.—is always right.

Coming to terms with what the Holocaust meant served to shed light on two centuries of errors and lies. No one can deny that the Holocaust, which was ordered by a positive law, beyond its horrible deeds sheds light on one of our most tragic intellectual errors. We now know that positive law cannot suffice unto itself, and that those who deny the existence of an unwritten law must urgently revisit their thinking. The Holocaust destroyed the legal positivism that issued from modern atheism. Late modernity is therefore marked by the trumpeted resurgence of natural law, even if it has returned in different garb. It is reassuring to see our contemporaries recover an awareness (which if possessed earlier would have avoided many evils) that laws exist which transcend the will of the leader, and even the will of the people, who are also quite capable of enacting unjust laws.

The contemporary idea of international justice is based upon a widespread indignation that gives rise to an absolute ethical certainty. How can one accept moral pluralism after the Nazi Holocaust and the millions of victims of communism? How can one claim today that we must let each people articulate good and evil as it chooses? Are National Socialism and communism each a "morality" like any other, born in determinate circumstances, based on specific customs and mores, and adhered to by a particular people and therefore, as such, respectable?

The century of totalitarianisms revived European universalism. It conferred upon it new titles of nobility. It also calls into question an earlier spirit of tolerance that had arisen to critique Christian missionary activity and European colonization. Who will extol such open-minded tolerance after Hitler and Stalin? Henceforth, the intolerable is here before our eyes, adequately revealing itself by its mere presence, imperiously admitting no further discussion concerning its status.

Of course, some people—many people—make a distinction between National Socialism and communism. They maintain that because Communist crimes were pardoned and not punished, and because communism left behind innumerable disappointed and unrepetant adherents, it is not communism that provides the basis for the new moral dogma, but only National Socialism. The Holocaust alone becomes the cornerstone that henceforth prohibits any vision of tolerance from being conceived or reconceived.

Thus is a hierarchy of good and evil dogmatically imposed, each type of conduct or historical action having to appear in judgment before it. The more that something approaches or resembles the Holocaust, the more satanic that something is. Our ad hoc international tribunals and the International Criminal Court (ICC) justify themselves in terms of their stands against genocide and crimes against humanity.

In this way, the Holocaust founds a new moral consensus. However, this consensus and this ethical certainty do not aim at articulating a complete morality whose teachings will be imposed upon all, as were the former, discredited moral teachings. One only needs to identify "the worst," forbid it, and seek to sanction it. One does not need to dictate a full code of virtues and vices. It therefore would be wrong, declare the proponents of the new moral consensus, to see in it a form of moral oppression. International justice only concerns itself with acts so monstrous that no one can approve of them. After what has happened in our times, who can blame so praiseworthy an intention?

And yet this attempt at an unassailable cogency is filled with tensions and contradictions. First of all, contrary to what it says or believes, this is *not* a universally agreed-to moral tenet; it is false, then, in the specific claim to universality on which it is based. Second, it is wrong to maintain without further discussion that doing justice in this way is *always* the best response to terrible types of crimes. It is not certain or even clear that in every case a brutalized society needs such justice to be reconstructed. And finally, this position does not appreciate how difficult it is to limit oneself to agreed-upon certainties, since the border between a "moral absolute" that one seeks to advance and the "morally relative" one seeks to preserve is not totally clear, as we shall see. In violating that border, the attempt to do justice provokes injustices.

Certain readers will think: It is impossible for any people to consider genocide, crimes against humanity, and war crimes to be "goods." Everyone without exception places these acts in the category of "evil." No one can deny this. There is no culture so barbaric that it takes the good for evil or vice versa, except in those times that we rightly call "perverse" or corrupt.

For this reason most of us will propose that international justice only punish universally recognized crimes. We will agree that it is not a form of cultural imperialism perpetrated by Western or European civilization, but something all peoples can agree to in their souls and consciences.

However, this affirmation is incorrectly conceived and misleadingly posed. The version posed by international justice is not: "Genocide, crimes against humanity, and war crimes represent monstrous crimes," but rather: "Genocide, crimes against humanity, and war crimes are crimes that are so monstrous that no ulterior purpose in the world can justify them." All peoples would agree to the first formulation, but not to the second.

For Milosevic, retaining Kosovo in "Greater Serbia" constituted a sufficiently elevated goal that it justified using means such as crimes against humanity. For Putin, maintaining Chechnya in the Russian empire justifies all sorts of crimes that, despite being somewhat veiled, nonetheless would have called down international denunciations if Russia weren't protected by its power, or rather by the fear and sympathy it inspires.

What distinguishes us from Milosevic and Putin is not that they do not recognize these crimes as crimes. It is that they pursue aims in the light of which these crimes appear to be justified. Between the advocates of international justice and its critics the debate is not over the criminal nature of the acts in question, but rather over the hierarchy of values that political action seeks to promote.

The advocates of international justice naturally find it outrageous that someone could justify crimes against humanity in order to keep Kosovo or Chechnya or any other territory within the borders of a political unit. In order to be understood, we will have to use an example they find comprehensible. Imagine that the Allies had the opportunity in 1943 to destroy the camp at Auschwitz. Should they have hesitated before the likelihood, even necessity, of killing or torturing combatants, even innocent civilians? And if the Allies had succeeded via these means in putting to an end the death camps, would we have wanted the generals who did so to be hauled before international courts of justice for war crimes? For us, I wager, the liberation of the camps would have justified such means.

(Nor can the advocates of international justice retort that it is acceptable to kill or torture Germans, who after all are themselves murderers. Remember: we here are dealing with a view of the world and of mankind in which every individual is worth every other, and in which human dignity is neither greater nor less depending on one's conduct. It does not allow for any sort of hierarchical ranking.)

It is probably because for a long time we have not known the exceptional case, the grave situation that imposes such Corneillan choices, that we simply assert the nonexistence of any event justifying such abominable crimes. We have forgotten that certain political priorities can demand sacrifices in terms of morality, because moral choice is never between good and evil but between two goods or between two evils. In truth, one must be utterly ignorant of real history to see things so simplistically.

Now, *we* could decide that the absolute avoidance of certain particularly odious crimes has become the absolute priority of *our* political life. That would mean that we were ready to suffer invasion, totalitarian rule, and oppression without ever employing against our adversaries this sort of immoral—what we deem "criminal"—activity. Is that realistic? On the contrary, if we found ourselves in certain dramatic situations even we would not hesitate to use the necessary means to defend ourselves—for example, if brownshirts showed themselves again, or if another sort of fanaticism reared its head, so long as it belonged to the broad category of those we abhor and detest.

Nor is this a hypothetical, a mere conjecture on my part. In Kosovo, in order to combat one of these criminal fanatics, we agreed to use—justly, we also said—certain means described by the Treaty of Rome as war crimes. For example, "launching a deliberate attack while knowing that it would incidentally cause loss of life and suffering among the civilian population" (art. 8). (Certain NGOs therefore accused NATO of war crimes. The ICC shelved the matter.) Now, some will acknowledge that we have used, perhaps, criminal means, but they will insist that we did so as a last resort against even more criminal acts. In this way, however, they indicate that criminalized actions cannot become *absolutely* illegitimate, which is what international justice wants to make us believe.

Even if we want to affirm that the avoidance of these crimes is the chief priority of our polities and policies, we cannot erect this into an absolute priority for everyone. Other peoples perhaps will raise other priorities above it, even if they themselves consider these acts as crimes. In a similar way, we can consider euthanasia to be murder but still commit it because of certain priorities to which we personally are committed. (This type of example shocks us because we have acquired the habit of removing the designation of "murder" from acts that appear to us to be sometimes justified. We do this in order not to dirty our hands.)

The question, then, is not whether we should leave unpunished certain actions recognized by everyone as crimes, but whether or not to allow different cultures to define their own political priorities. For international crimes, despite what we have a tendency to believe, are not opposed to the good but often to evils considered rightly or wrongly as worse.

In addition, one might ask, is rendering justice for acts that everyone not deprived of elementary humanity agrees are monstrous the *only* form that the desire to restore civic concord can or should take? Is it *the* response to evil, so imperiously obligatory that no people can prefer another to it?

The effort to create international justice is tantamount to applying the famous Latin sentence: *Fiat justitia et pereat mundus*! Let justice be done and let the world perish! The press release of the first condemnation of Radislav Krstic by the International Criminal Court* began as follows: "Let justice be done, or the world will perish, as Hegel said. . . ." That

* Radislav Krstic (b. 1948), chief of staff/deputy commander of the Drina Corps of the Bosnian Serb Army from 1994–95. In 1995, he was promoted to general-major and assumed command of the Drina Corps in July. In 1998, he was indicted for war crimes by the International Criminal Court for the Former Yugoslavia. Found guilty, on appeal his conviction was overturned, although the appellate court upheld the lesser charge that he was an aider and abettor to genocide.

is a very different translation, or version, of the famous phrase, which means: "Let the world perish, just as long as justice is done!" It was in an exposition of Fichte's philosophical system that Hegel denounced the absurd extension and destructive application of law found in that maxim. "It does not mean, as it does for Kant, *let justice reign even though all the rogues and scoundrels in the world have to perish*, but rather: justice must be done even if that requires extirpating by the root all trust and confidence, all joy, all love, all the resources of a truly moral identity."[1] Here, as in another passage of the *German Constitution*, Hegel shows that a justice that makes itself the sole finality of action is blind and implacable, that it destroys life itself without any compunction.[2]

It can happen, and it often happens, that a society which has been brought to its knees by monstrously criminal acts prefers amnesty to justice because it sees in amnesty a better way to preserve future social concord. Who can decide in its place? Who can blame it for this decision, one in which all the wounds of the past are taken into consideration together with the possibility of reconstructing life in common? Do we have to castigate the Cambodians if they decide not to prosecute Pol Pot's thugs?

Rather curiously, when we French saw the Romanians abstain from judging Ceaucescu's crimes, we enthusiastically applauded and ritualistically intoned the following commentary: the Romanians must feel that they all are more or less accomplices, therefore for social harmony it is better not to judge. In other words, a kind of respect that consists in allowing a people to provide for its own reconstruction resonates with us when it is convenient. After all it was not Roman—or French—legionnaires but Communists whom the Romanians declined to judge.

After the fall of the Berlin Wall the countries of Central Europe made different decisions concerning their former tormenters. The Czechs voted for the law of "lustration," which temporarily excluded from public life the former elites. In fact, it was the question concerning justice versus pardon, among others, that divided the Czechs and the

Slovaks. The Poles and the Hungarians preferred pardon (one cannot speak of simply forgetting). Who of us would dare from the sidelines to pronounce on either decision? As for the supposed counterexample of the Nuremberg trial, please note: The Nuremberg trial was the decision of *Westerners* confronting *Westerners* guilty of horrible crimes. They were deemed to share common values and thus to be subject to common standards. In this light, I do not agree that one must understand the trial either as an act of vengeance or, at the other extreme, as God's verdict. It was the desire and will of a continent to open a new page for the sake of its own future.

In any particular situation, only the person concerned can know what should be done. In *The Music Box*, a 1989 film in which Jessica Lange stars, a trial takes place involving a Hungarian refugee accused of committing Nazi crimes during the war. He is found not guilty, but his daughter discovers undeniable proof of his guilt. Despite her love for him, she decides to bring the evidence to court so that justice can be done. This is a personal choice, and in that regard it is respectable, but it cannot be institutionalized. Whether, as in this case, it is a matter of a *family*'s cohesion, or whether we are speaking of a people or a country, only the agents themselves can decide if the full application of justice should become a priority or not. Only they can decide if it will facilitate the return of concord or rather prevent it.

The architects of international justice say or imply that when states do not put *Fiat justitia* first they are merely following their particular interests, which, as such, are dubious at best. For example, Antonio Cassese writes: "The sovereign state has a tendency to pursue its short-term interests, all too often to the detriment of the general interests of the international community."[3] Or Carla Del Ponte, the procurator-general of the International Criminal Court, in a talk given at the École Nationale d'Administration (ENA) in June 2003: "Most states are more concerned to maintain a precarious equilibrium based upon the doctrine of sovereignty than to pursue criminals against humanity." However, "short-term interests" and "a precarious equilibrium" only appear to be such because they are opposed to an eternal ideal enthroned in the heaven of ideas. States and peoples live in historical time and must concern themselves with their own existence and continuity, even if these are tainted by imperfection. It was a realistic appraisal that made Emmanuel Decaux† say, "I am not an absolutist about justice." One must be prepared to accept that sometimes justice has to be sacrificed—put into parentheses—for the sake of certain political considerations, including the avoidance of a country's disintegration.

Put another way, the question to ask is not how to post and display the (purportedly) agreed-upon list of abominable crimes, but whether "the world"—the staying-together of a society—should be sacrificed for the sake of justice?

International justice also reveals itself to be more dogmatic than it acknowledges, since it is unable to keep to punishing truly monstrous actions and actors. Remember: it wants to respect the liberty of each people to establish its own moral norms in keeping with its particular culture. It wants to be tolerant except with regard to the few acts that it decides it no longer will tolerate, acts the nature and boundaries of which it defines: genocide, crimes against humanity, and war crimes. It has decided to distinguish between absolute moral norms, which as such are beyond any question or discussion, and norms that are relative to various cultures, which are to be tolerated even when they appear to us to be cruel or inhuman.

The problem is that the boundaries separating the absolute from the relative are vague and moving. Immoral actions do not divide themselves clearly into two kinds, genocidal (or crimes against humanity) and all others. There are many immoral actions about which one is unsure whether they fall into the former category or not, or whether they should be identified with what has been designated as objective evil, the new foundation of moral dogmatism. Many agents have participated more or less in the incriminated actions. It is hard to tell whether to include them with those who are fully responsible, because their responsibility is

† Decaux is a professor of international law at the University of Paris–II.

diminished, indirect, only "shared." In an important movement—and moment—that helped found the new moral universalism, Westerners identified Serbian misdeeds as crimes against humanity and Milosevic with Hitler. But how should one categorize the war Sharon led against the Palestinians? The Nobel Prize winner for literature José Saramago has declared that the Israeli operations conducted in the Palestinian territories are comparable to the crimes of Auschwitz, a claim that gave rise to the protests of many. On the other hand, Amnesty International claims that the terrorist acts of some Palestinian groups are crimes against humanity.

Elsewhere, certain organizations committed to the defense of human rights demanded that NATO be summoned to court because of the bombardment of Yugoslavia. General Janvier just missed being charged with not having stopped the Srebrenica massacre. And should one call to judgment the police forces throughout the world who fire on crowds? The list could be extended.

What is obvious for the Holocaust stops being so as soon as a court established to address an exception becomes a permanent institution—that is, as soon as one has to establish gradations of evil. So many different problems and considerations are involved, the number of criminals is so great, the situations are so different, the terrain of horrors so unexplored. Many nuances have to be determined concerning degrees of complicity: one needs to differentiate giving commands from allowing something to happen, cynicism from indifference, and so forth. There is the well-known criminal, the chief author of the carnage—and glad of it to boot. Then there are the underlings. The accomplices. The satellites. And those who did not want to see or know. There is obedience to a criminal state (sometimes hard to define) versus obedience to a legitimate state that history later judges to be criminal in certain regards.

And how far do we go in identifying purported crimes against humanity? The *Washington Post* asked whether the immigration policy of the United States bears comparison with crimes against humanity. Why? Because the wall proposed to stop illegal Mexican immigration leads to deaths in the desert. One eventually finds oneself in a situation characterized by constant accusations. Everyone judges everyone, and more and more crimes are likened to the Crime. Recently, *fifty* world leaders were the subjects of accusations, from Sharon to Fidel Castro, and including Hissène Habré of Chad, Driss Basri of Morocco, George W. Bush, and Yasser Arafat. The number can and will be extended. When everyone is guilty, law loses its relevance and becomes rather ridiculous. If we want these sorts of deeds—which, alas, are rather widespread in the world—to become, as we say, *unacceptable crimes*, then what really happens is that we ourselves become unrealistic and crude in our judgments.

In these ways, the recognition of an objectively intolerable event—intolerable no matter what the situation, no matter what the circumstances—opens the way to general *intolerance.* For the world is not black-and-white but rather a mix of clarity and obscurity.

The existence of an "intolerable-in-itself," something objective and unquestionable, allows or leads one to discern criminals everywhere by comparing them with the acknowledged model. But dogmatism only has to be legitimated on a single point—that we must be intolerant in the face of the Holocaust—for it to become legitimated everywhere. One only has to liken an act of war to the truly intolerable for it to become itself objectively intolerable, and thus the subject of a (purportedly) universal judgment of condemnation. This likening, however, is a matter of interpretation, of sentiment or passion, of belonging to a particular camp or side. In the pro-Palestinian demonstrations in Paris in April 2002, we saw written on placards "Sharon = Nazi." As soon as "the evil in itself" is marked out, a type of mind appears that knows how to find it everywhere by means of assimilation and amalgamation.

It is obvious that all forms of justice, not just international justice, run into this difficulty. Rape is a crime under our law, but in a number of cases how can one determine whether a rape has occurred or not? The determination is left to the judgment of judges or juries. In these cases, though, the judges are scrutinized by their neighbors and fellow citizens. If they sometimes make excessive or erroneous judgments, they cannot do so with total impunity. But in the case of international justice, *it* is the ultimate judge, and it is moved or swayed by currently dominant world opinion, itself full of enthusiasm for *Fiat justitia*. What truly godlike wisdom must the members of the International Criminal Court possess lest they commit false identifications, questionable assimilations? Won't its members have a tendency to compare their *own* enemies to the Devil rather than restricting this comparison to those who truly are enemies of the human race? This sort of judgment is difficult once one leaves behind extreme cases. And in life we are not faced solely with extreme cases! We encounter a multitude of more complex, more ambiguous cases, before which the human mind is perplexed.

That is why we even have difficulty clearly recognizing actions ostensibly belonging to the three types of international crimes. These types "are imperfectly defined," said Claude Jorda, president of the ICC: "Article 5 of the statute on crimes against humanity speaks of *other inhuman actions* . . . , which is a sort of *catch-all* category."[4] And even in extreme cases, does the crime present itself with equal evidence to everyone? No, because even though Nazi crimes and those of Milosevic appear to be objectively unacceptable, indulgence accompanies the crimes of communism without our being able or willing to say how they are less obscene than the former. The fact that certain genocides, that of the Ukrainians for example, elicit an irritated silence clearly shows the subjectivity of the judgment involved. That entire families, including children, are disposed of in gas chambers in North Korea does not interest us very much. Because our judgment is itself steeped in historical circumstances we cannot really grasp an absolute morality.

As soon as a breech is made in our tolerance, the intolerable can gain a foothold everywhere. We cannot be dogmatic on only one point and tolerant on everything else. We cannot say, one cannot kill Jews but one can kill Armenians. We cannot say, one cannot kill Jews or Armenians but one can fire on demonstrating crowds. International justice rises to forbid and punish genocide, crimes against humanity, and war crimes. That is, it proscribes not war itself but the monstrous excesses of war and politics. Who, however, can define the boundary between the monstrous and the acceptable?

Some will respond: Do we therefore have to relativize everything, since we cannot draw a line between the absolute and the relative? Do we have to become accomplices to crimes because we do not want to become inquisitors? No. There is a way out of this impasse. Because an absolute norm cannot be precisely defined, one should refrain from institutionalizing it. Not to tolerate certain crimes ought to be a *decision*, not a matter of obedience to positive law. If in matters of such gravity the borders are indistinct, it belongs to conscience and not the law to mark them out. This, at least, is the position I want to defend.

CHAPTER 4

THE CONTEMPORARY DISMISSAL OF MONTESQUIEU AND THE MODERATE ENLIGHTENMENT

IN *THE SPIRIT OF THE LAWS* (1748), Montesquieu effected a revolution, one that called into question the character of Christian missionary activity and the legitimacy of Western colonization. He took it upon himself to understand the different laws of different peoples in their own contexts. He described and explained them in their own existential milieu, instead of judging them in the name of a dogma or teaching that transcended all of them.

To be sure, human laws are inspired by morality, they "legislate concerning the good."[1] However, the vision of good and evil varies—considerably so—according to each people. The resulting moral differences are founded upon liberty. It is in freedom that each people designates the good, which is to say that a variety of factors enter into account: its way of life, its religion and culture, its mores and manners (the two are not the same), its climate, etc.

All human laws are therefore inscribed within a given context, and they should correspond to a distinctive interpretation of the world in general and of morality in particular. "They must be so fitted and appropriate to the people for whom they are made that it is a great matter of luck if those of one people can suit another."[2]

Is Montesquieu's argument relativistic? One might think so, reading certain passages he penned on despotism. In them he lets it be understood that, as Aristotle said before him, natural servitude can be good for certain peoples.[3] Elsewhere he writes: "Do not compare the morality of the Chinese with that of Europe."[4] We will see a bit later, however, that Montesquieu is not a relativist, even if Christian authorities of the period were quick to say so because he rejected the dogmatic point of view that consecrated a single vision of the good as true for all peoples. In fact, Montesquieu hewed to a narrow and complex path between relativism and dogmatism. He does not fail to identify universal laws applicable to all human beings—no one is more keen than he on the unity of the human race—nor does he fail to connect law and morality. But these two convictions prompt him to abandon the regnant dogmatism. And in point of fact these two convictions correspond to the two historical foundations of tolerance.

The first conviction consists in regarding the search for the good as a probabilistic activity, one that is always tied to a specific situation. In this sense, morality as a practical activity connects with the Aristotelian notion of prudence. The definition of the good is always uncertain because it has to be articulated by human beings with less-than-perfect minds who are immersed in particular situations from which they cannot attain total critical distance. Without existing in *some* particular situation they don't have a world at all. Therefore, it is very difficult to judge a law or custom in absolute terms. For example, with respect to polygamy: "It is clear that there are countries in which there are many more women than men. Therefore polygamy, which is bad in itself, is much less so in them than in other countries."[5] This uncertainty in the definition of the good corresponds to the modern foundation of tolerance, found for example in John Locke's *Letter on Toleration*. Here it is the uncertain character, the weakness of human judgment, the diversity of human demands, which call dogmatism into question.

The second conviction concerns the dignity of peoples and hence the respect due to their customs and cultures understood as expressions of their particular ways of life. Montesquieu insists a thousand times that "peoples are very attached to their customs."[6] To want to change from the outside the laws of a people because of the barbaric character of those laws is to make them one's slave.

> Moreover, since one likes to establish elsewhere what one finds established at home, [this nation] will give the peoples of its colonies its own form of government . . . ; although it gives them its own laws, it maintains them in great dependence; in such a way that its citizens will be free there, but the state itself enslaved. A conquered state might have a good civil government; but it would be oppressed by the law of nations: the laws of one nation will be imposed upon the other in such a way that whatever prosperity it achieves will be very precarious, and really only held for the use of the master.[7]

In other words, maintaining the autonomy of a people is worth more than getting rid of its imperfections. It is very possible that we could bring better laws to certain peoples than they currently possess. But in doing this we would annihilate that people along with its laws. That is why Montesquieu was so exercised that an Indian king was judged by the laws of another people and not his own. This argument concerning the dignity of peoples—despite the fact that some of their laws appear to us to be unworthy of humanity—corresponds to the classical Christian foundation of tolerance found, for example, in Saint Augustine. In this argument it is respect for the other that demands that dogmatism be eschewed.

Westerners today ought to meditate upon Montesquieu's admirable reflections whenever they decide to launch a war of humanitarian intervention. These reflections especially call into question the institutionalization and systematization at work in contemporary demands for international justice.

Montesquieu's thought casts doubt on some certainties or tenets of the Christian religion. The author of *The Spirit of the Laws* claimed that, even if its truths are universal, the church cannot disdain all the different laws that do not accord with its truths. The churches therefore vigorously attacked him. The Jesuits did so in the famous *Mémoirs of Trévoux*, followed by the Jansenists in their *Nouvelles ecclésiastiques*. This led to Montesquieu's own "Defense *of The Spirit of the Laws*."

This debate was remarkably exemplary and premonitory. We do not do anything different today in the name of human rights than the church did in Montesquieu's day. The dominant doctrine has changed, but the spirit undergirding it, the spirit of domination, remains the same. It thus appears that the considerable progress in toleration accomplished in the interval has been lost or eradicated. *The Spirit of the Laws* itself would be poorly received today—if, that is, anyone read it. Montesquieu is a man of the Enlightenment in the sense that he defends the capacity of each people to conceive the good by, and for, itself. Our attitude toward him reveals our attitude toward it.

In his little work *What Is Enlightenment?* Kant shows that the Enlightenment—or rather the process of enlightenment, if one takes the German word *Aufklärung* in its literal sense—means "the vocation of each human being to think for himself": *sapere aude*, dare to think for yourself. To do this entails a disengagement from every imposed dogma. No truth can henceforth be deemed so certain or so objective that it rules out autonomous freedom of thought.

The ideologies that arose in the nineteenth century and were given concrete form in the twentieth marked the beginning of the calling into question of the Enlightenment through the betrayal of its principles. It was now in the name of "true" or "real Enlightenment" that constraint was justified—the new *compelle intrare*, compel them to enter. The certainty of having scientifically discovered an objective good naturally led to a denial of the ensemble of thoughts and modes of being that refused to enlist under its banner. In the name of Progress and Reason—

which he believes he has thoroughly grasped—Condorçet rose up against Montesquieu, the defender of pluralism. "Since truth, reason, justice, the rights of man, and the interest in property, liberty, and security are the same everywhere, I do not see why all the provinces of a state, or even all states, would not have the same criminal laws, the same civil laws, the same commercial laws, etc. A good law ought to be good for all men, just as a true proposition is true for all men."[8] Moreover, Condorçet was persuaded that the secret hope of all peoples is for this uniformization: "The ideas of uniformity, of regularity, please all minds, especially right-thinking ones."[9]

In the same vein, Anacharsis Cloots looked forward to the advent of a "fundamental truth" in the name of which a uniform or "leveled universe" would be organized.[10] Rivalries and wars would be suppressed and the Republic of the entire human race would abolish all borders; even the words "stranger" and "foreigner"—"barbaric expressions of which we are beginning to be rightly ashamed"—would disappear.[11] Cloots did not hesitate to say that "the universal Republic will replace the Catholic Church . . . theological unity produces only evils, political unity will produce only goods."[12] The old dogma is therefore not critiqued because of its monopoly but because of its content, and another monopoly will replace it. Enlightenment understood in this way has for its goal the leveling of the human world, and later totalitarianisms would embody this movement. The will to establish "scientific socialism" announced by the First International* revealed the reintroduction of dogmatism, this time in the name of science rather than religion. And it was partly in the name of science that National Socialism sought to impose its certitudes. Because the International considered its vision of the world to be objectively true, it believed that it could legitimately establish itself anywhere in the world, by any means.

International justice and world government are the most recent expressions of this vision of things. The search for a world government continues in the path of the discredited totalitarianisms. The filiation

---

* See page 3.

cannot be doubted. What they have in common is the unity of doctrine and power, the absorption of all differences by a center, and the denial of plurality. The old demon of leveling and homogenization resurfaces at every opportunity; it is always present even if disguised. To be sure, the idea of unity is beautiful to behold and embrace. This is why the search for the world state has such deep roots and emerged so long ago, as well as why it will not simply go away. In order to make it go away, human beings—all of them—will have to be truly reasonable, and not merely rational.

But someone might retort: Do we really have to believe that the true spirit of Enlightenment as described by Kant has once again been betrayed? With totalitarian ideologies gone, aren't human rights taking the place of discredited and banished dogmas? Not really. To desire global justice and therefore world government is to affirm that only one political truth exists, which is objectively certain and which therefore should legitimately be imposed upon all peoples. It is to believe that one group of people—as a matter of fact, we Westerners—can establish the truth in the name of all other human beings, and can impose it because of the certainty that it is right.

In these discussions it is as if what is unacceptable about totalitarian ideologies is solely found in the content of their claims—racial or class superiority. But what is truly unacceptable is found in the idea of an absolute certainty, of an objective truth in the name of which one can coerce consciences and bodies. We easily see this point when we compare the totalitarianisms of the twentieth century with the Inquisition, their precursor. Tzvetan Todorov is right to make a comparison between the war in Kosovo and the crusades, or even the colonial wars of our forefathers.[13] He sees a regression in our current manner of seeing ourselves as the sole possessors of the good, "as in the wars of religion. They ceased, in principle, the day that it was admitted that several conceptions of the good can coexist."[14] The acceptance of pluralism represented a considerable advance in terms of civilization, that is, in terms of respect for *the other*. Today, this civilizing advance is being called into question. We seem to be returning to the period before Montesquieu—a return, to be sure, undertaken with the best of intentions, and which believes itself to be a victory for humanity. What is the secret of this paradox?

CHAPTER 5

THE MONOPOLY ON MORAL JUDGMENT AND AN INTERNATIONAL MORAL ORDER

THE DESIRE TO establish global authorities charged with judging and punishing responds to the monstrous perversity of certain states. Ideologies tasked politics with regenerating humanity. Instead, they terrorized and decimated humanity. States charged with the care of the common good used their powers to destroy the populations in their care. In the face of these perversions of politics, morality assumes precedence and wants to assume the role of governing men. It will take the place of the state and arrogate to itself the state's authority to legitimately judge and punish. International justice effaces the distinction between law and morality. It seeks to institute an international moral order.

With the collapse of their earthly visions and hopes, morality substitutes for the ideologies of criminal states. It both assumes political attributes and claims to transcend politics, because politics allowed itself to be perverted. In so doing, however, it borrows the characteristic form of the ideologies it replaces and thus represents their continuation or prolongation. Just as was the case with the defunct ideologies, in the struggle conducted under the banner of human rights the adversary is deemed *guilty*, this time not because he belongs to a certain race or class but because of his *immorality*. Thus, war conducted in the name of human rights has nothing in common with the old wars for territory or power. It is like wars of religion or ideology, which aimed at those who were guilty rather than simply at the enemies of the group. Hence its efforts not only to judge criminals but to demand repentance from them, to extract confessions, which is what was done in both the Inquisition and in ideological regimes. Hence, too, its tendency toward Manicheanism, which is the exaggerated form that all moralisms take when they attain power, because power does not allow for half-enemies. In the same way, moral powers cannot imagine "half-guilty."

International justice does not seek to establish truly democratic procedures in trials. Such procedures institutionalize and put into relief the difficulty in establishing guilt. That is why trials consist in a debate between opposing parties: one can never know in advance if the accused will be found guilty or not. It is in the sham courts of the Inquisition and ideological regimes that the accused is found guilty before judgment. "No, no," says the Queen in *Alice in Wonderland*, "first the sentence then the deliberation!" Or in Kafka's *The Penal Colony*: "The principle according to which I judge is that guilt is always beyond any doubt. Other tribunals cannot apply this principle because they have several judges and other, more important, courts above them. This is not the case here."

The same happens in the case of international justice. Years ago, Hannah Arendt noted that Eichmann had been already considered guilty before his trial, which is why "his illegal arrest could be justified."[1] Antoine Garapon noted that "treating Maurice Papon as though he were innocent, which is what the rules of the trial require, became intolerable to certain civil parties."[2] He shows how some persons justify or excuse these derogations of justice by the "enormity" of the crimes being prosecuted. As an observer of the International Criminal Court said: "The guilt of the accused, even if it gives rise to several questions and is the issue at the origin of the Court's mission, is rarely called into question. There is a willing omission in connection with the accused, and an extreme care is taken to produce the following result: the accused is guilty. The primacy of facts over persons is flagrant—the Court judges events above all. . . . The tribunal does not allow the accused a real voice and attempts to do everything to foreclose the result of the process: the declaration of guilt."[3]

We cannot act like Lewis Carroll's Queen except if the accused is the Devil incarnate. As we know, the totalitarian regimes demonized the accused before making them appear in show-trials. On the other hand, no crime should call into question the great formality (and humility) that ought to inspire a democratic trial. Would the mothers of the Belgian children who were tortured by Dutroux require, because of the horror of the acts, that he be formally accused before any deliberation?* The immense pain of some victims allows us to understand certain isolated acts of vengeance, but as soon as those victims agree to participate in a civil process they must adhere to the democratic process requiring witnesses, evidence, plausible narratives, etc., before conviction. Neither opinion nor rumor suffices to convict a man.

If international justice has such a difficult time respecting these democratic processes it is because it is more a *moral* tribunal than a legal one. Although law is inspired by morality, it represents a mediation of morality and power. By its forms, procedures, and debates it moderates the (potentially) great violence of any power that wants to judge directly in the name of morality. Only law casts doubt and raises misgivings, allowing us to see that the world is grey rather than black-and-white. Democratic institutions—hard-won achievements—are the fruit of the desire to place law between morality and power.

It is therefore rather curious to observe Europeans declaim against the Manicheanism of the United States. The vengeful or threatening speech of George W. Bush against "the axis of evil" can cause one to smile or even become alarmed before a simplistic view of the world, one that is

* Marc Dutroux (b. 1956) is a Belgian serial killer. His widely publicized trial took place in 2004.

ill-suited to its complexities. We, however, exhibit the same simplicity when we identify Milosevic with Hitler or, worse yet, Berlusconi with Mussolini. With us, too, states are divided into "rogue states" and "virtuous states." The same holds for different governmental programs, as Alain Lipietz somewhat inadvertently shows. "If one attempts to realize the genuinely 'virtuous' program but in an insolated way, won't 'vice'—that is, all the others who do not follow that program—triumph, especially in a globalized and competitive world? In this context the real question is, how can one attempt to protect virtue and contain vice?"[4] The "virtuous" program of the author is "to increase the quality of life and leisure time" for all. This moral vision of the world, which was characteristic of premodern ages, proceeds as if the Enlightenment never happened. It is a civilizational regression.

In this context, Serbia, Austria, and Italy under Berlusconi are the rogue states of Europe. And Hungary received a warning during the elections of April 2002: it would become an immoral state if the extreme right party was rewarded for assisting the election of Victor Orban.[†] And so on.

The absolute certitude with which we assign good and evil indicates just how much a true pluralism of judgments and attitudes, a sense of nuance, a civilized hesitation before the difficult judgments of moral practice, are deserting us. Like the Jacobins of yesterday, we have begun to instrumentalize morality in order to make it a political weapon. This is the gravest of our errors. No one has the right to instruct another in morality, unless he is a director of consciences. Nor, a fortiori, can one coerce another to adopt or act in accord with some morality. Without liberty of conscience morality destroys itself. If we become the spiritual directors of the entire world—a role we currently attribute to ourselves—it can only be by reestablishing a monopoly on moral judgment, a monopoly that the Enlightenment broke only with great difficulty.

It is not surprising, therefore, that the accused countries rise up. Such was the case in April 2000, when 122 developing countries

† Victor Orban (b. 1963), Hungarian politician, prime minister of Hungary (1998–2002).

condemned the intervention of the powerful in their affairs under the pretext of a "purported right of humanitarian intervention."[5] When Westerners deem it necessary or merely desirable, change of behavior is imperiously—should I say, imperially?—demanded of other countries.

This recalls any number of abuses of authority by the powerful. Kafka's tale of a certain father, for instance. Whatever the father decrees is the good to which the entire family has to agree. But when he changes his mind they have to do so as well. His edicts are arbitrary and temporary. His family is whisked from one criterion to another.

In other periods of history, Europeans have decreed that power alone counts, but today it is morality. In earlier times they wanted industrialization; today they want to protect the environment. In every case, though, the world has to follow suit, no matter the circumstances in which others find themselves.

The desire to monopolize judgment is a natural tendency of ancient peoples, a tribal reflex when they encounter others. The true greatness of a civilization emerges when it begins to accept that others exist who are also capable of thinking and judging. This was the merit of Herodotus, the Greek who in the fifth century before Christ wrote his *Histories,* which presaged Montesquieu's great work. Rather than *we* and *the barbarians,* Herodotus recognized that there are different peoples whose differences make it difficult for them to accept one another and easy for each to treat the others as barbarians.

To abandon the idea that one has a monopoly on thinking and judgment is a sign of a more advanced humanity.

Monopoly is connected with the thought of *perfection*. Men advance as they renounce the thought that they are perfect. In a formula, monopoly is solitude in the singularity of perfection. The monopoly of judgment to which international justice aspires requires the uniqueness of perfect judgment since there can be no other judgment as true. But is that true? In the current system, the International Criminal Court can only take up a case when national courts fail or refuse to do so. But what would have happened if Serbian courts had judged that Milosevic was innocent?

Diversity, in contrast, is synonymous with imperfection. It also implies a form of disorder.

To monopolize judgment is a permanent temptation for man. He can stop himself from doing so only with the greatest of difficulty. This monopolization is easy to justify to oneself before one comes to know or recognize others. This was true, for example, of the ancient tribes who called themselves "The Humans," because they were convinced that *they* were the only truly human beings on earth. All others with whom they were acquainted were "barbarians." In these persons they did not recognize humanity, at least not to the same degree.

The desire to establish a world court, and then a world government, corresponds to the perceived necessity of transcending the power of particular governments when they commit crimes. A new power that is capable of trumping otherwise independent sovereign powers must be created. Political sovereignty must therefore be called into question and held responsible for its deeds. Who today would deny the legitimacy of this effort? And yet it involves a contradiction. In order to transcend the various political sovereignties, it institutes a monopoly equivalent to a supersovereignty. One can—and must—ask: will it always decide and act justly? If not, who will come to the aid of those whom the organs of global justice might persecute? Do we believe that these institutions and their personnel will be "always good," like Plato's government in the *Republic*?

It is neither a divine being nor even Moses who designates such-and-such action as criminal, but rather powerful NGOs who have no democratic mandate but rather are the self-proclaimed representatives of all humanity. It is an international judge who, in the midst of various notions concerning crimes against humanity, will decide according to "the idea that he has . . . of the values that are common to humanity." In so doing he "exercises a veritable creative power."[6] It will always be the judgment of imperfect men, neither better nor worse than others, to whom we have committed the task of pronouncing the absolute norm. And it has been a very long time since we have placed such trust in either a priest or a king. It is reminiscent of enlightened despotism: since we are defending human rights, the judge cannot err. In the same way, we formerly thought that if the king was "good" we could give him all authority. Our certainty concerning the objective good cannot but engender such enlightened despotism. If the good is known, why allow debate to occur? Why attempt to harmonize diverse opinions? For us, human rights are like the law of Moses: since they have come down from heaven, why discuss them?

The same people who demand international criminal courts are up in arms about the extent of American power, which is now capable of spanning the globe. Their anxiety is legitimate. It is not good that all power should be held by a single set of hands, because those hands always will eventually disappoint; as Lord Acton said, power tends to corrupt, and absolute power corrupts absolutely. Every monopoly in the human world is on the path to corruption, to perversion. That is why Europeans have always essayed to divide power. Only this kind of diversity has allowed us to slow down, if not exactly to avoid, many catastrophes. If a free world had not coexisted with them, National Socialism and communism would probably still exist—unless one had by now devoured the other, which would not be much of a consolation.

The aspiration for international justice implies a rejection of modernity in the sense that modernity could cast doubt on and relativize its own certainties. Perhaps it entails a sort of return to the status quo ante. How can this be, you ask, since we are talking about an idea held to be the most innovative, the most progressive—a culmination, a fulfillment, of various historical dreams?

I return to Montesquieu. He wrote at a time when the dogmas of the church were still legally enforced. He does not reject them. He contextualizes them. But the dogmas (and their adherents) claim to transcend space and time; they rise up against his procedure. Montesquieu, for example, had written that there are countries "where natural slavery exists."[7] To be sure, as we saw earlier, he certainly recognized universal laws founded on human nature. However, he assigns two senses to "nature." "As all men are born equal, one must say that slavery is against nature; however, in certain countries it is founded on a natural reason."[8] The Jesuits and the Jansenists replied in indignation: This is unacceptable relativism! You thereby justify terrible practices—slavery, polygamy. . . . Not at all, responded Montesquieu. I do not justify them, I give the reasons why they exist. Now, are certain practices so intolerable from the point of view of natural law that to explain them is tantamount to justifying them? That is what the church thought.

In the sixteenth century, nations colonized in the name of civilization. How could one allow uncivilized peoples to commit such atrocious crimes? One European wrote: "Each day, moreover, four or five Indians were sacrificed before us, and their hearts were offered to idols. Their blood spattered the walls, their legs were cut off, as well as their arms, so that they could be devoured like meat in our butcher shops. . . . After having seen so many cruelties and indignities we no longer had the patience to forebear. . . ."[9]

Montesquieu appears attractive to our time because of what he destabilized: religion. But he would be as shunned by today's clerics as he was by those of his own day.

Montesquieu saw *processes* where the church saw *essences*. Later modernity, however, did not emulate him. It hastened to reconstruct new essences on the tombs of those it destroyed. Montesquieu's innocent gaze, devoid of prejudice and fixed on the reality of societies, did not survive modern rationalism. This rationalism, "like Midas, is always in the unfortunate position of not being able to touch anything, without transforming it into an abstraction."[10] Secularized Western universalism began with the revolutionary era. It produced new dogmas. As Michael Oakeshott said, the principles of human rights were held to be "not the products of civilization; they were natural, *written in the whole volume of human nature*."[11]

Hence, a new essentialism took the place of the old religious essentialism. Normative principles, especially those rights of man which demand respect, came to be seen as "self-evident," inscribed in nature and reason. The two in fact go together: healthy reason discloses true nature.

International justice purports to judge crimes outside of the context of politics and positive law, outside of culture and custom. It judges what we can call intrinsic crimes, indifferent to history or geography. In this way it has nothing to envy the church, which roots itself in unchanging, eternal sources. International justice, though, has this advantage over the church: it can impose its norms precisely because they are not its own. They were discovered in the deep soil of a *nature* considered as a permanent *state*. In fact, they are not imposed; they impose themselves. So say its proponents.

The contemporary aspiration for international justice thus announces the appearance of a new and very dogmatic religion. The new one distinguishes itself from the old one by its content and, as we have seen, by the ground of its doctrines.

By its ground: its dogmas no longer are established on the basis of their *truth* but on their *valence*, their attractive and repulsive force. International justice appeals to a consensus of repugnance. That is why it is unsuccessful in designating clearly the point of intolerable abusiveness that it charges itself with indicting and punishing. The monstrosity of a crime depends rather on the force of the indignation generated in spectators. How can we explain the indulgence shown the crimes of communism, if not by the fact that our subjectivity helps determine the intolerableness of acts?

But the content of dogmatic norms has also been transformed. This difference between the old religious essentialism and the essentialism of human rights is found in the notion of the "natural." What is "self-evident" is not the same in the two dispensations. The norms that reason cannot deny do not have the same content. Robert Spaemann calls this "an inversion of teleology," as the values that formerly were located above and outside the individual have been internalized. Spaemann finds particularly present in Thomas Campanella (1568–1639) the root of this change from external to internal finality. This new ontology, which Spaemann calls "bourgeois ontology,"[12] corresponds to what we today call "the loss of meaning" in life. It has paradoxically itself become the meaning of life. There no longer exists any goal or aspiration outside of life itself. In late modernity the biological life of the individual has acquired the status of supreme value, to which every ideal, value, or idea must be subordinated or sacrificed.

This inversion has a philosophical pedigree—it can be traced to Rousseau, to give a well-known example. It appeared massively and influentially in post–WWII texts. "Save bodies!" cried Camus in *Neither Victims nor Executioners* (November 1946). Contemplating the terrorism of grand ideas, the massacres committed by "heroes" endowed with "higher purposes," he wrote: "My conviction is that we no longer can reasonably have the hope of saving everything, but we can at least propose to save bodies, so that the future remains possible."[13]

The dogmatic character of the contemporary demand for international justice, whatever its foundations and content, also shows itself across the *diversity* it rides roughshod over. It therefore neglects the criteria of what we ordinarily understand by justice, at least insofar as it remains *human* justice.

CHAPTER 6

LAW AND RECOGNITION: A PRESUPPOSED BUT NONEXISTENT MORAL CONSENSUS

THE CONTEMPORARY DEFENDERS of world unity commit an error of judgment that goes to the very nature of politics. They imagine that one can compensate for the dismantling of particular societies by replacing them with universal laws, as if a world order could take the place and fulfill the role of the faltering states. In fact, the one cannot be replaced by the other, because they belong to different orders.

Every positive law is rooted in a culture. Therefore, in order to have a world law there must be a world culture. And there is no such thing.

Together with its sanctions, a law cannot be legitimately enforced unless it is widely *recognized and acknowledged* by those to whom it applies. Positive law presupposes societal recognition because it is drawn from a common culture, a common ethic. It does not descend from heaven. If it comes from a tyrant—whether domestic or foreign—who has no regard for local customs it immediately becomes terroristic. There is nothing more striking and distressing than the guilty verdicts issued by totalitarian governments: they often surprised the "guilty," who did not know *why* they were guilty.

In the context of contemporary international law a number of criminals declare themselves "at a loss"; these individuals plead "not guilty" because they do not understand why they are accused by the particular court in question. Christian-Nils Robert describes a "stateless 'orphan court,' one without roots." It is "composed of exotic—foreign—judges" and of accused who are "cut off from the discussion because *officially* one does not speak their language." This is capped by a "foreign prison for the condemned."[1]

The legitimacy of law, on the other hand, is founded in its appropriateness for the culture to which it applies, that is, upon societal acknowledgment. Of course, one may ask if the legal or societal denial of something—a crime—destroys its reality. Of course it doesn't. But the decisions of international courts are deprived of social legitimacy. Each positive law is a particular attempt to embody the just, but no law is perfectly just. For this reason the application of a law and the sanction that accompanies it require the agreement of those to whom they apply. We would regard any Arab Muslims or Chinese who attempted to judge us according to their laws as terrorists. This, however, is what we are trying to do with international law.

In *The Penal Colony* Franz Kafka described a scene of this sort. We see a condemned man about to be executed. He looks at the execution machine with curiosity, as if it were prepared for someone else. He does not understand his death sentence and can make no sense of it. The feeling of injustice grows in the reader with each page.

A state naturally has a responsibility to assist its people in progressing to a higher stage of civilization. This is what we hope will happen by obtaining the agreement of more and more peoples to conventions of this sort. But the state ought not to apply to its people laws they do not understand—in other words, it ought not to try to civilize them by imposition, paternalistically. For in doing so it denies the very dignity it is otherwise attempting to honor. Kant wisely wrote: "In constructing a bridge men can defer to an expert without degrading themselves. However, religion and law pertain to, and concern, each human being as such. That is why no one in these areas can content himself with deferring to a specialist. If he does, he remains in his immaturity and he abdicates his dignity as a human being. If the rights of man depended upon clerics, the liberty of most men would be at the mercy of a caste that would not fail to keep them ignorant so as to maintain them as long as possible under its yoke."[2]

The law in totalitarian states did not seek to be socially recognized because it embodied an ideological truth designed to transform human beings who otherwise would be left behind in history. It was a law devoted to *creating* a society, not to *serving* it. A positive law that would apply to all the peoples of the earth would inevitably resemble such a law. It could not appeal to the common recognition of cultures that are so different. Therefore, it would apply to purported criminals in the way that Kafka's sentence did.

Because of this reality, some have insisted on the requirement that international justice can only apply to states that have recognized its authority and competence.[3] However, many signatory states in fact signed on to various conventions because of diplomatic pressure from Western powers. In general, they do not attribute the same gravity to "crimes against humanity" as do we. This is why the most powerful non-Western states, Russia and China, have refused to sign. Therefore, even in the case of signatory nations, most criminals will be judged according to laws that do not derive from their cultures. Article 12 of the Treaty of Rome concerning the International Criminal Court is particularly troubling in this regard. At best it speaks like the enigmatic Sibylline oracle, but it also intimates that in certain cases the court can exercise its authority even on a nonparty state.[4]

Too late, but still sincerely, Western conscience differentiated the Holocaust from other mass crimes committed elsewhere and even previously. This crime was committed in the bosom of a culture that later was gripped by remorse, and this for the first time in history. It was not the Nazi criminals who felt remorse, but rather Europe and the entire West. They felt that they had prepared, even nourished in their midst, National Socialism—via the eugenicism of the late nineteenth century, the words of hatred uttered by authors of all persuasions, the anti-Semitism harbored even in the churches.

The novelty therefore lay less in the cruelty and inhumanity of the twentieth century—which were horrible enough—but in the remarkable *denunciation* of those cruelties and in the declaration of their inhuman character. It seems to me that it is the emergence of this consciousness (and conscience) that constitutes the true and also unique character of the Nuremberg trial. It also should prevent us from wanting to establish a *world* court on the same model.

In 1524, shortly after Cortez's bloody conquest, a dozen Franciscan friars disembarked in Mexico to convert the natives to Christianity. We come in peace, said the friars to the Indians. Why, then, the Indians replied, have men of your people massacred us? The friars answered: God knew you were sinners; it was lawful to kill you. . . .

In contrast, the Nuremberg trial was prompted by the West's horror before what it was capable of producing. For a crime or misdeed that pertains to the moral—not the legal—order, only the one who is responsible for it can judge himself. The only Western tribunal that could follow the precedent of Nuremberg would be one that considered the crimes of communism. The West as a whole invented, sheltered, and justified communism; therefore, it can rightly feel culpable and can judge itself. This second trial, of course, is impossible for two reasons: Russia's power, and the impenitence of former European Communists of all nationalities who feel neither responsible nor guilty. In this case the obtuse West does not feel that it created and sheltered a monster.

Thus, Nuremberg represents a unique instance in which all the requisite circumstances for an unprecedented trial came together, including an unwritten law that condemned those who had followed a written law. The trial was made possible only by an act of conscience and by the remorse of an entire culture. And this act of conscience was itself made possible by a comparison of the Nazis' criminal acts with the moral convictions espoused and nourished by the very same culture: the notion of human dignity, first, and that of human rights, second. If mass crimes are always crimes against the human, they still cannot come to conscience as crimes except when the society responsible for them is marked by those cultural conditions which make possible recognizing them as such. Peoples who, as it were, have practiced "collective murder" forever and have legitimated it by their ways of life and thinking cannot immediately become aware, simply on command, of the inhumanity of this practice.

In this regard, international justice adds an additional difficulty to justice at the national level. Not only must one pay attention to the personal situation of the criminal but also his cultural situation. In any given society the cultural situation is, in principle, the same for everyone: each person has been raised to refuse to commit certain acts and to recognize the reasons for that refusal. International justice must take into account the fact that crimes are not assigned the same gravity in every country. One cannot punish with the same severity Aristotle, who possessed slaves in a slave-owning culture, and a Westerner who today owned slaves. What is true in time is also true in space. One cannot judge in the same way a Rwandan criminal who has inherited a bloody history and customs and a Western war criminal, born after fifty years of reflection on totalitarianism.

This does not mean that the gravity of crimes is simply relative to the situation in which they are committed. Any crime against humanity is universally grave, whatever the time or place. But the person who commits it, his personal situation and his cultural situation, must be taken into account. Our judgment of *him* will vary accordingly.

It seems to me, then, that if Nuremberg was justified by the remorse that a culture felt when confronted with its own development, the European tribunal that recently judged the massacres of Rwanda cannot claim the same legitimacy. In the absence of its own conscientious remorse, we see here a sanction applied from the outside to a people who do not understand it.

Within a civil society it is well known that "no one is deemed ignorant of the law." This is why a retroactive law seems so unjust, for it entails punishing someone who did not know what he did was wrong. To judge the criminals of Rwanda is to apply to them a retrospective law. The people who set up Nuremberg knew that the criminals had violated a law that they themselves recognized. Hence their horror.

Echoing in our own way Kant's argument, we love to believe that the nation-state, which put an end to the natural warfare between rival individuals and groups, can be extended to a world state, which would do the same for states. It is a seductive argument. One must take note, however, of the way in which the emerging nation-states arrived at establishing common laws over territories with longstanding conflicts. They did so by obtaining, sometimes with great difficulty, the recognition of the legitimacy and justice of the state by all concerned parties, often having to instill this conviction over a long stretch of time and by all sorts of means. The new nation-states removed entire territories from the anarchy of the state of nature not only by force but by framing a justice acceptable to all.

Analogously, international justice and the world government which is its corollary must rest on universally recognized norms. Without them it must use coercion everywhere to compensate for the nonrecognition of these norms. In this way it will lead to constant war.

If international justice wants to avoid being a new religion, if it wants to avoid any return of dogmatism, it must speak in the name of a truly consensual morality, one held by all the peoples of the earth. If a universal justice does not want to incur the reproach of colonizing consciences, if it does not want to impose itself as a moral order—thereby destroying its morality, because morality requires liberty—then it must really judge in the name of all cultures.

And if a world government capable of applying a universal law wants to escape from despotism, then all peoples, at the same time that they legislate for themselves, have to give themselves the same law. On the conditions that one will not impose a foreign law and that one wants a universal law, there must be a free convergence of all peoples toward the same law.

In other words, the aspiration to international justice entails a search for the universal morality underlying all cultures.

Have we discovered such a foundation in human rights? This would be the sole valid claim justifying a law applicable to all peoples. One can believe that in the name of the unity of the human race a universal morality is present under apparent diversity. Mireille Delmas-Marty, for example, asks, "[I]s it not toward the victims that one must turn to seek universal values despite the different, even conflicting, civilizations?"[5] Unfortunately, I do not believe this to be true. It often takes centuries for victims to appear as victims even to themselves: Marx showed this with the proletariat. I do not believe that Muslim women in general are conscious of the anomalous character of their condition, except when they find themselves in zones of contact between different cultures. To recognize an evil requires a progress of conscience that sometime takes centuries and is sometimes initiated by those Bergson depicted as the heroes of the universal.

In the sixteenth century, in order to complete his project for "world harmony," William Postel sought the universal law, norms approved by all peoples because they are inherent in the human spirit, inscribed both in our reason and in our nature. One does not have to look long to notice the ascendancy of the particular over the purported universal in his case. First of all, the universal law did not arise among all peoples at the same time, as one might believe, but from the author's own perspective. We will obtain world harmony, he said, on two conditions: all peoples will have to convert to Christianity, and they will have to subject themselves to a universal head, the French king! In order for that to happen, one must first employ persuasion and kindness. But if that does not succeed? War. So Postel did not discover a universal law present among all peoples; he decreed the religious and political laws of his country to be universal. That is, he had in mind the laws of his own time, which he erected into absolutes. Much more has been written in this same vein.

According to Postel, the first two sources of justice are the fear of God and property rights. Could one find more historically contingent norms than these? If proposed today, wouldn't they make us laugh? Today, though, Frenchmen and -women are convinced that their own particular arrangement concerning religion and politics, the emphatically secular state, should be a universal law, which is why they attempt to impose it via various European charters.

Condorçet and Anacharsis Cloots were also convinced that they had discovered the universal laws by which humanity could advance toward happiness and peace. These laws, however, came from Europe and more particularly from France, the most "enlightened" country.[6] From there they would radiate and extend over all the earth. In a similar way, as Tzvetan Todorov nicely showed in his book *Conquest of America: The Question of the Others*, Saint-Simon and Comte sought a world society founded on universal norms whose point of departure was France and Europe.[7]

Also in the same way, when the Commission of the Bishops of the European Union recently produced a report on world governance they spoke of "an ensemble of fundamental values and principles that must be accepted." They added that "the Church offers its social teaching as the definition of values and principles for a system of world governance."

A universal morality has to be the foundation upon which world norms are based. However, this universal morality always has its origins in European particularity. This takes away not its credibility or its value, but its right to impose itself.

We cannot free ourselves from particularity. No human institution can represent adequately the universal. It is dubious when NGOs claim to be the spokesmen par excellence of justice. NGOs advocating for international justice are partisans like any other group of humans. They are dangerous not because they are partisans but because they claim to be objective.

These agencies and institutions justify their advocacy in the name of natural law, a universal law purified of particular prejudices. They base their legitimacy on a convergence of views that has not yet been realized. One can hope that in time the governments of China and Borneo will adopt laws that, recognizing human dignity, serve to ground human rights. That time, however, has not come. The cart has been placed before the horse, presupposing what history has not yet brought about.

Yesterday's dogmatisms, whether religious or ideological, effected the same substitution. The beautiful wager of *hope* becomes oppressive when it justifies coercion in order to hurry along or compel history's slow-footed march.

International justice thus remains steeped in the particularities it so ardently desires to transcend. It is not the rule of international law that it imposes but rather the rule of hidden particularities. International justice is still a matter of human power and authority, which no one can overcome. We can only dissimulate. Justice that wants to free itself from politics is still political. But it operates clandestinely, does not avow itself, and hides under the guise of the universal. It therefore is a politics that is more arbitrary and more dangerous than others: Why indict Pinochet rather than Castro?

We cannot truly aim at the universal without also acknowledging the *particular*'s place and status. The search for unity should not take place to the detriment of *diversity*, which also possesses its legitimacy. Because it violates both, we should consider world justice and its correlate, world government, as highly undesirable.

CHAPTER 7

BABEL AND THE FEAR OF THE FRAGMENTATION OF THE WORLD

THERE ARE TWO ways of interpreting the story of Babel. The first consists in emphasizing God's jealousy. Here is a united humanity all speaking the same language, the sign of living together. In order to protect their unity they decide to build a tower: "Let us make a name for ourselves and avoid being dispersed over the earth." Seeing this, the Eternal is disconcerted: "Behold, they are one people and speak the same language, and this is but the beginning of their endeavors. No design will be impossible for them. Let us go down and divide their tongues so that they will not be able to understand one another." In this way, the Creator himself puts an end to their common enterprise, dispersing humankind and causing human diversity. One is inclined to say that he feared being equaled, perhaps even surpassed, and that he used his power in order to maintain his creatures in a position of inferiority.

This interpretation springs from a Promethean vision: man can do anything, but the gods are jealous and disrupt his projects in order to maintain their monopoly on omnipotence. However, in the context of monotheism a God who is jealous about his supremacy is not really

God. That is why the story of Prometheus, worked out at the time of multiple anthropomorphic deities, logically produces atheism when it encounters monotheism. If God is jealous then he does not exist.

The story of the tower of Babel, therefore, cannot be identified with the story of Prometheus, even if one sees in both stories the irrepressible human desire to overcome the constraints of man's limited power. The story of Babel situates itself in the context of transcendent monotheism, not the immanent polytheism of the Greeks. Here God is unique and beyond the world, indefinable except by his "perfection"—the understanding of which still eludes us. It would be most unfitting to attribute feelings of jealousy to him. The story has to have a different meaning—unless one wants to attribute no meaning to it.

The biblical God could not have dispersed men except in view of a positive good, one favorable to them. What appears as a disruption must be understood as a benefit, or at worst as a lesser evil. In so acting, the biblical God wanted to spare men the untoward consequences of their ill-conceived design. Hence we need to seek for another interpretation.

The tower of Babel no doubt was inspired by the cultic towers—the ziggurats—of Mesopotamia. They were considered a connection between heaven and earth, the gods and men. The children of Israel encountered them, or their ruins, during their journeys. The towers symbolized the hubris of polytheistic peoples given over to the immanence of the divine and thence to idolatry.[1] In this light, the biblical story is more anthropological—more about man and human nature—than it is "religious." It seeks to indicate the proper stature or true measure of man, which only the transcendent God, in his transcendence, can put into relief.

The question we raised earlier is nonetheless apropos: What is the benefit that can justify the dispersion of mankind? This is a particularly pointed question because traditionally, for all cultures, evil meant separation—*dia-bolos*—while unity always declared itself as a good. One does not immediately see the danger in a collaborative endeavor, one undertaken in mutual understanding and for a common ideal of unity. One does not see the benefit of the separation and dispersal of men to the four quarters of the earth, one that begins with and requires the confusion of tongues.

The question posed by the story of the tower of Babel is this: Why, and when, is diversity legitimate?

There is an anthropology detectable in the biblical text, an anthropology that through the centuries remained that of Christian civilization. An answer to the question can be drawn from it. In this anthropology, man is viewed as a being who becomes, who is never fully completed but is always becoming so. In other words, he is a being with a beginning and a finality. Since one can only tend toward the good, or what one believes is good (that is the very definition of the good), man is the imperfect being who imperfectly directs himself toward perfection. This perfection, however, is not found in this world. It presents itself as a desire or hope to which every creature called "man" aspires. Man in fact is compelled to such hope because he is unable to cause perfection to reside here. His true dream is not directed toward that which is here below.

In this earthly realm, therefore, a "perfect" unity could only be a false unity. To repeat: What characterizes man is not any unity that is finally, perfectly, achieved, but the activity and effort undertaken in view of unity, the action by which he progresses toward communion without ever completely realizing it. The effort expended in view of and for the sake of unity can be expressed in a single word: relation. The task and work of man on earth consists in weaving relations between diversities. This is the way he evolves and grows in stature. Individually, moral life consists in developing human relations between different personalities who are respected in their differences. Collectively, the search for unity passes not through the abolition of cultural differences but by their constant maintenance or sustenance. To become civilized is nothing other than to learn to genuinely recognize the *other*. In the story of Babel, the other as such was suppressed, since each person had lost his *differentiation*.

Differentiation expresses specificity. If being loses its specificity, it loses its dignity. The biblical anthropology, and later that of Christendom, ties the value of being to its unique singularity. Any unity that sought to dissolve these singularities would ipso facto abolish its own value. This is why God prefers a harmony to a unity, "a providence that still has not been appreciated," writes Erri de Luca.[2] On the other hand, the desire for unity is deep-seated and potentially violent. The totalitarian regimes expressed it. In Orwell's world only one language, one thought, one form of conduct exists. Such Prometheanism revealed itself in the perversion of Enlightenment thought found at the time of the French Revolution. It envisaged the unification of the world in terms of universal values universally applied.

In his *On the Spirit of Conquest and Usurpation* (1814), Benjamin Constant wrote at length, and ironically, about the modern passion for uniformity.[3] "The admiration for uniformity, a very real admiration in some quite limited minds, and feigned by many servile ones, was and is received as a religious dogma and is constantly seconded by repeated echoes."[4] The will for uniformity is a permanent indicator of "empire" and "the spirit of conquest." It appeared stronger than ever during the Revolution. In this connection, Constant underscored the paradox of a doctrine that under the banner of liberty wanted to impose the same view of the world everywhere. He was well aware—as are we—that the revolutionary ideal is much closer to enlightened despotism than to democracy. This ideal involves forcing people to be free according to its own definition of freedom. Constant, in contrast, insisted on the reality and legitimacy of peoples' different lives: "Variety is organic, uniformity is mechanical. Life is variety, uniformity, death."[5] As Montesquieu had pointed out earlier, uniformity requires perfection, a perfection not to be had.[6]

Perfection, in fact, is the key word. It is what Ernst Jünger feared, this perfection "which renders freedom superfluous."[7] We have so much difficulty "tolerating plurality"![8] We ceaselessly level the sexes, states, classes, in what is called "the triumph of the norm" or "normalization."[9]

This process was advanced during the latter part of the twentieth century as a sort of exorcism of the bloodshed experienced during the earlier "wars of particularisms" involving nations, races, and classes. In Jünger's view, the universal state appears to be an irresistible destiny, one tied to the disappearance of particularities and to the globalization that accompanies it.

Nonetheless, one must note that the hope for unity is also a concrete desire, a legitimate desire, one that human history brings to effect. The transition from the tribe to the nation lifted individuals and groups out of their particularisms and allowed them to begin to recognize the other. The polytheism of local gods, ancestor gods, gave way to the monotheism that unified mankind under a single deity and gave credibility to the idea of a single human race. And we never stop seeking universal moral laws, inscribed in each human being. Each relapse into separation—into hatred and segregation—leaves us upset and ashamed.

The desire for unity characteristic of our human condition and destiny is never stronger than when efforts at separation, at dislocation, appear. The present moment is one of those times when separations have developed. The world of the twenty-first century is fragmenting, "re-feudalizing," while the great empires collapse and the tutelary social-welfare states erode. Great fear and apprehension accompany this apparently ineluctable process of fragmentation, which has been provoked in part by the excessive rationalization and unification that followed previous periods of fragmentation.[10] The history of the world oscillates between order and disorder, between the dominion of empires and the anarchy of multiple wars, between stability and instability. Stability and order require a powerful power. It is likely, even predictable, that this power leads to the draining of passive obedient souls and to the encouragement of dissident energies. We live today in such a period. The totalitarian regimes, on the one hand, and the social-welfare states, on the other, have for too long penned up particularisms. The latter now are ready for the adventure of disorder. In the face of this prospect the call for unity is made in the shrillest tones. The desire for unity, which after all is so human and issues from a legitimate ideal, finds itself strengthened even more during those historical moments when societies seem on the brink of exploding.

CHAPTER 8

PLURALITY AND LIBERTY: THE BENEFITS OF CONFLICT

THE HISTORY OF European culture recounts the acceptance of diversity as the condition for the freedom of differing interpretations of the world. When the world is only understood from a single perspective that takes itself as the sole truth, man believes that he lives under the reign of the True and the Good. This, however, is only an illusion, which European doubt has taken upon itself to critique and unmask over the centuries. When Aristotle defined politics as the governing of plural liberties, he exposed the hyperbole that lay behind any government's claim to be endowed with wholly objective knowledge that knows the Good without any discussion—the government described in Plato's *Republic*. With the age of Enlightenment we see the appearance of doubt, or a departure from the closed world of certainty. The various Copernican revolutions from Galileo to Freud undermined conviction in certain basic truths. Modernity is the moment when people perceived that every purported truth is an interpretation of the world and not the veritable mirror image of it. Man's spirit took on the disparate character of these interpretations. He agreed to live in a pluralistic world in which interpretations confront one another and do battle.

As we have said, Enlightenment is falsified when its adherents believe that they have entered, and can make others enter, into the single universal truth. The evolution of this perversion runs from the enlightened despotism of Voltaire to contemporary discourse concerning international justice. In contrast, true Enlightenment is an expression of the awareness of uncertainty. Paradoxically, it signifies that humanity has entered into an awareness of shadow, doubt, and particularity. Particularity means "a part that does not pretend to be the whole." The true destiny of Enlightenment is to accept the plurality of cultural worlds, because it is aware that no single culture is capable of alone grasping the whole truth.

One must not conclude from this that the truth consists in the mere addition of various points of view. There certainly are interpretations that are more accurate and adequate than others. And some by the damage they have caused have demonstrated their falsity. We nevertheless have to recognize and admit that we cannot directly encounter the truth, and that our convictions attach themselves to interpretations which, as such, are necessarily plural because they translate different perspectives.

The plurality of interpretations of the world—in other words, the diversity of cultures—does more than reveal the impossibility for men to define the truth (or the good) independently of particular mediations. It does not merely reveal a limitation in his means, or a limit of his being (at least vis-à-vis that to which he aspires). It expresses essential features of the human condition concerning man's freedom and his evolutionary or developmental character.

Diversity alone can guarantee liberty. It is likely that respect for diversity of principles—including territory—was the essential factor that allowed Europe to invent political liberty. François Guizot noted this in 1846: "While in other civilizations the exclusive dominance, or at least the excessive preponderance, of a single principle, of a single form, was the cause of tyranny; in modern Europe the diversity of the elements of social order, the impossibility of one excluding the other, gave birth to the liberty that reigns today."[1]

Only the existence of multiple definitions of Justice can allow us to escape the dictatorship of a single one. The particularities of politics—of distinct views of justice and different states—are the only guarantees against the demiurgic temptation inherent in the desire for justice. To be sure, each political form believes it is universal even though it is never more than particular. But it can only be stopped in its pretensions by other particularities that rise up in its way. An international justice that encountered no obstacle would soon take itself for God.

The plurality of cultures shows how humanity finds itself in a *process* and not as a finished state. Plurality is the necessary condition of mobility. A culture or a government that was alone and unique in the world would have little opportunity, or need, to change or transform itself. No one seeks to change except by imagining something better than himself, by comparison and contrast. The Berlin Wall aimed to eliminate possible comparisons, as well as to stop the exodus of those who had made the comparison. Ignorance of the real other allows one to believe that one is perfect. A country that believes itself the best by nature—like France—changes only with great difficulty, because every comparison with another seems to be an insult. Where, then, can it find the image of something better?

Europe owes its prodigious development to the diversity of its cultures, to a pluralism that exists within a relatively small space. Each time that a government in Europe approached tyranny, its best minds escaped and went to think—and criticize—in neighboring countries. A scientific or institutional discovery made in one country immediately attracted the attention of others—who then imitated and appropriated it. Galileo used glasses from Holland to make a telescope, Montesquieu presented the English regime to the French as the model of political liberty. No one can find in himself alone all that he needs for his own perfection. In fact, a culture that believes it has found the Good will remain stationary. But the human world is not made for immobility. Deprived of any principle of self-motion, such a culture does not really have the option of remaining immobile in its unchanging beauty:

it necessarily will become corrupt. There is no choice but constant reformation. This occurs only through constantly calling itself into question—and through the acceptance of others.

It is rather curious to see contemporary Europe renounce the critical spirit, Europe's own discovery, which is envied by the elites of so many other countries. Listen to Middle Eastern writers. The Iranian Darius Shayegan: "Democracy is the child of Enlightenment. And Enlightenment is the apex of the critical age. That is, the merciless critique of dogmatic truths. . . . We need to learn a certain humility, a certain relativity of values . . . to liberate ourselves from this mad egocentrism which seems to suggest that the world begins and ends with Islam."[2] Or the Lebanese, Selim Abou: "Totalitarian practices show their immoral character in comparison with democratic values. . . . [O]ne cannot insist too much on the importance of critical thought which historically was at the origin of modernity and of democracy and which remains today the necessary condition for their emergence in non-Western countries."[3]

The suppression of comparisons casts one into solipsism and schizophrenia. Monopolistic thought stumbles about under the megalomania of its own passions. It believes it is perfect, so others become superfluous. It chokes on its own pride. Only others' gazes, others' opinions, limit the excesses of thought, relativize it, and impose upon it its own critical gaze. Continual progress in the human world necessarily passes through the acceptance of comparisons. Every unchallenged monopoly of thought petrifies.

Our contemporaries hardly admit or deign to consider the Taliban as an "other" who belongs to the concert of cultures. Rather, the Taliban are a cancer to remove, a disgusting relic of a bygone age. That is, we prefer to make such a culture toe the line of a universal law rather than to authentically tolerate them or, eventually, to fight them. Because we deny them a true "alterity," we prefer to treat them as common criminals rather than as partners or adversaries. In fact it is often to avoid these conflicts that we have a tendency to deny such "otherness." Otherness is pregnant with potential conflicts.

For if the other exists qua other, all sorts of relations are possible between us, from friendship to war, passing through an infinity of possibilities and nuances. War naturally represents a horrible sort of relation, one to be avoided as much as one can. But it still is a relation in the sense that the other is recognized as such. Contrary to what one might at first think, the Americans' treatment of Iraq—their invasion of Iraq—is more defensible than what Westerners did to Serbia. Whether rightly or wrongly, the Americans judged the Iraqi regime to be dangerous, invaded, and overturned it. On the contrary, NATO did not officially declare and make war on Serbia, but instead conducted a police operation aimed at the elimination of a criminal. But a police operation finds its legitimacy within a given society, one internally structured by laws connected with its distinctive culture. (No state can allow *all* modes of thought and behavior.) The *plurality* of cultures means that only war can respond to the intolerable. At the international level, a police operation is a refusal to consider the other as other. Serbia (or Milosevic) is considered not as the other but as *what ought not to exist.*

Conflict represents one of the existential conditions of a diversity worthy of the name. He who hopes to definitively suppress conflict desires at the same time to definitively suppress differences. The contemporary ideological mindset naturally interprets the acceptance of conflict as the tolerance of, or even as a cynical attitude toward, war. This is why Samuel Huntington is so disdained in France.* But the acceptance of the possibility, even likelihood, of conflict does *not* exclude the patient search for peace, much less the love of peace! On the contrary, it is easier to deal with a phenomenon when one recognizes it rather than simply denies it. Pacifists sometimes cause even more terrible wars, as we saw in 1940.

Some like to praise the animals who, they observe, do not fight wars,

* Samuel Huntington (b. 1927), the Albert J. Weatherhead III University Professor at Harvard, is a prominent American political scientist. His intellectual interests and works range widely. He has written on military-civilian relationships, global democratization, politics and culture, and civilizational conflict.

except to eat. But it is because they are without culture that they do not enter into conflict. Do you want to suppress culture in order to suppress quarrels? "If we lived in a perfect community," wrote Proudhon, "our civilization would be a stable."[4] And Kant: "Like an Arcadian shepherd, men would live in perfect concord, contentment, and mutual love, and all talents would lie eternally dormant in their seed; men docile as the sheep that they tend would hardly invest their existence with any worth greater than that of cattle."[5]

Very true. Man cannot live beneath the level of conflicts, because he is not an animal. Nor can he live "beyond" conflicts, because he is not a god. Being—existence—exposes itself in conflict, but the distinctiveness of a culture only exists in its self-manifestation, in its putting itself forth. A culture does not develop except by exposing itself to the gaze of others, to judgments that come from *elsewhere.* Because of this fact, the evolution of the human world is fueled by irritants and friction, and advances by fits and starts.

Moreover, only a diversity of points of view allows the development of individual conscience. In a monopolistic vision of the world such a conscience hibernates unmolested; it knows nothing of the critical spirit. The monopoly of a sole norm leads in short order to the triumph of the norm over conscience. Persons do not truly develop except in the midst of a plurality of norms. Every monopoly kills life.

The realization of world unity by means of international law, it is true, would respond to a legitimate hope. If we only criticized and simply denied this hope, we would be compelled to simply accept conflicts between particularities. But its realization runs up against human diversity. Hence the deeper question: Why should we protect diversity instead of trying to erase it in unity? Why should we accept a diversity of ethical points of view, which itself engenders a diversity of laws, and which risks allowing visions of good and evil that we find to be inhuman to assert themselves?

"Plurality is the law of the earth," wrote Hannah Arendt.[6] That is true, but a mere description does not suffice. All our history testifies to the effort to transform given reality into something more livable. There is no reason to merely describe what is and then to make it a norm. We have to ask, what justifies protecting diversity? What that is humanly important, even essential, does diversity ensure?

Human existence remains an enigma. The thinking species is destined to tragedy, in the sense that the questions it eternally poses never find a definitive answer. What is the answer to questions like: Why death? Why evil and conflict? What is justice? The deepest meaning of culture is to propose partial, provisional, or temporary answers to these queries. Man is the animal that interrogates his existence. The diversity of cultures characterizes humanity because humanity poses to itself questions that in their nature are finally unanswerable. Human existence, in other words, is an enigma, not a simple *aporia*, a "pathless" condition. Human existence is not an impasse; rather, it opens up multiple ways to respond to these eternal questions. This is what creates those fissures, so hard to accept, between humans who are simultaneously alike in their common "tragic" condition and different in the paths they tread as a consequence of such questioning. Only someone who had definitively resolved the enigma of human existence would have the right to unify and homogenize cultures. But this uncontested superman does not exist, even if during the past two centuries several have tried to personify him.

If men's aspirations are for unity and perfect peace, then, as Kant remarked, nature fortunately separates them by means of different languages and religions. Why does Kant praise the nature that separates? Because it prevents "liberty's cemetery." Their differences prompt men to seek peace and unity—but in an equilibrium of differences rather than in the enervation or annihilation of their wills.[7] The necessity of a plurality of cultures, moralities, politics, and religions thus is rooted in man's very being. He responds freely, and therefore variously, to the questions that pose themselves to him, especially the question of good and evil. Pluralism—diversity—is liberty's ransom, the sign of man's finitude. Man can choose the responses he gives to the enigma of his existence, but he can never discover *the* definitive answer.

CHAPTER 9

LIMITS: THE CONDITION AND GUARANTEE OF DIVERSITY

IT IS TRUE that the will for unification (and even leveling homogenization) that emerged during the French revolutionary period and still manifests itself in the effort to establish international justice does not in general claim to abolish all differences, nor does it aim to produce perfectly laid-out utopias. The desire to save what can be saved of human diversity remains. This is the case today with the advocates of world government. They do not want to eliminate all cultural differences. In this regard, our era is remarkably like the eighteenth century, which was also marked by a similar sort of reasoning that aimed to reconcile the irreconcilable.

For Anacharsis Cloots, only those laws which bear upon essentials are applicable to all, for example, those pertaining to monogamy.[1] On the other hand, as long as they do not violate natural universal laws, each people ought to retain its own customs: "Differences of customs, cultures, and worship do not disturb the social harmony."[2] What this really means, though, is that diversity will remain in the form of *folklore*. This is what the French Republic did when it forbade speaking the Breton dialect in schools but said students could wear regional dress on designated days. Or the Chinese Communist regime, when it outlawed ancient matriarchal customs in the Yunan province while organizing in its capital various holidays celebrating "traditional customs." These efforts make manifest what we already know: the expressions of a culture form a whole. Every aspect is significant. The recent headscarf brouhaha in France showed this clearly.* The veil signifies a submission, a choice not to act in certain ways, even a self-imposed concealment, beneath which an entire world is contained—and affirmed. If one separates cultural expressions from their foundations, from their structuring frameworks, they are transformed into dead letters. In fact, this is what we mean today by "folklore."

Therefore, we should not think that we can establish, as it were, partial universal laws that leave intact essential cultural values, or that leave each people otherwise free to govern themselves as they please. Even if one changes the formula and says that one only will outlaw "the intolerable" and leave the rest to free choice. "The intolerable," as we have seen, cannot be defined precisely. It will be found everywhere, in everything, by someone. All peoples will finally merely be left with disconnected folktales.

Only plurality guarantees otherness. There have to be "differents" for there to be "others." This truism needs to be repeated today. And relations—upon which human being-in-the-world wholly rests—are only made possible by otherness. Identicals neither see nor talk to one another. Would I really speak to my image in the mirror? The common world disappears without relations. That world depends upon a space that allows for the existence of different beings, a space that simultaneously allows their differentiation and connects them. There has to be some distance—in fact, separation—for rapprochement to occur. Even similarity presupposes difference in order to appear. Speech requires silence, search, a felt absence.

The all-too-frequent error of our times is to believe that the abolition

* Since 1965 France has been a rigorously secular state. All expressions of religious belief are forbidden in public institutions, including public schools. Recently, Muslim girls in France sought the right to wear burkas (headscarves) to school, in keeping with their Muslim faith.

of limits will lead to the abolition of divisions between countries, human groups, the sexes, etc. We dream of a universal harmony between human beings and societies without significant differences. The contrary is true. In-differentiation is a terrible constriction, a deadening closing. Who needs another, who wants to know about another, if he is simply like you and everyone else? This mode of thinking operates at more than the personal or interpersonal level. We are told that to refuse to admit Turkey into the European Union because it is Islamic would be a shameful act of discrimination on our part. In other words, the straightforward acknowledgment of deep differences between us and them is taken as an insult.

Have we become incapable of entering into relations with those who are different? Of speaking to "the other" without disdain or irony? Do we have to assume that every recognition of difference means loathing it? The will to create a perfect world will always reappear as long as we believe that evil is simply whatever separates, and the good, what unites. In this view, every difference, since it inevitably contains the possibility of conflict, has to be overcome in order to attain a perfect unity of wills, which is the sole tangible realization of the good. This is why the apostles of perfection in this life always demand the leveling and even the suppression of diversities. They have not grasped what is really in humanity's power (and they never will, because this temptation occurs in each age, albeit under different forms). What is in humanity's power is not perfection but improvement. The two belong to two very different orders.

Humanity, it is true, *can* seek the good understood as the unity of wills. No one can say that it cannot happen, but only that humanity itself would then disappear. We perhaps can create the utopia of a thoroughly egalitarian society, with peace reigning along with international law and world government. But at the same time one would see that those rendered "happy" or "satisfied" in this way would be terribly diminished. This is because of a mystery inherent in human existence. For human beings to exist, *differences*, real *others*, have to be accepted and relations with them entered into. Existence itself is only given in the mode of continual development; immobility destroys it—even the immobility of perfection. (Whether one can really define "perfection" is a separate question.) Human existence is incompatible with both perfection and death, which in some sense are synonymous.

Gilbert Durand therefore writes that one must always begin with imperfection if one wants to enter the sole path worthy of man, the path of improvement or perfectibility. If one begins with perfection, one is compelled to eradicate evil wherever it is found, and thus to enter into bloody worlds. He elaborates: "When one first posits imperfection, in order to draw from it its lessons—and *not* by beginning with the arrogance of some envisaged perfection—what results is not properly called a perfection but rather 'plenitude.' The idea of perfection that asserts itself as a program really aims to destroy its negation, imperfection. It is 'the sin of angelicism.' Imperfection that is self-aware also posits otherness and *its* existence, as Descartes said."[3] Human life desires plenitude more than perfection. And plenitude requires that one not neglect the shadows, what is not oneself, the other, the enigmatic. Human existence does not develop except by being deeply connected to these enigmas. Death, evil, the other: all represent enigmas whose constant examination expands being.

On the other hand, the rejection of pluralism and thence of otherness reveals a form of Manicheanism. Everything that is an obstacle to the anticipated perfection must be removed, and for that one must sharply distinguish good from evil and place entities squarely in each category. In contrast, the plural world teems with nuances. The other is not reducible to evil but approximates to or else is remote from it. In each case one's knowledge and understanding of the world are enriched.

But because contemporary European universalism wants to realize here and now the Pauline ontology that grounded the unity of the human race, it tends to deny *boundaries*. It does so either to abolish them or to turn them into *bridges*. It sees the differences between cultures as ancient relics that have to be abandoned, because all human beings on earth are destined to adopt the same reference points and to live in accordance with the same model, that of human rights. To this way of thinking the very notion of *limit* appears as an affront to progress and to the universal that both guides progress and is its goal.

One of modernity's main characteristics is the rejection of limits. It is natural that *those who desire to remake themselves* would object to the barriers that previous philosophies have erected. In innumerable currents of thought and in different ways modernity wants to strike down the limits that stop man from becoming what he wants to be. Evil, for example, is a limit that restricts our will to power because beyond its limits we become inhuman. Gender is a limit that stops us from equating, from identifying, male and female. Our contemporaries are doing everything to abolish this difference, hoping thereby to create an androgyne. The human condition itself, endowed with all the traits that characterize it, represents a limit that governments and societies can abolish only at the price of creating an uninhabitable world.

The European universalism now at work is the continuance of this sort of modern thinking; it presses its postmodern agenda on the basis of modernity's presuppositions. In contrast, premodern universalists from Saint Paul to Las Casas never thought that the universal could be realized in this realm, much less here and now. Rather, they saw it as the *foundation* of an ontological perspective and the *horizon* of a practical point of view. According to them, the universal that founded the Christian epoch could not be entirely realized in this world because the limits of the human condition were ineradicable. On the other hand, it represented humanity's *hope*, for humanity's character resides precisely in the fact that it is not satisfied with given reality. For two centuries now we have been convinced that *all is possible*. It is therefore unsurprising that even today, in the wake of various wrongheaded doctrines and disastrous efforts to re-create man, the universal still is not taken as a hope but is demanded as a reality. We therefore must abolish all limits, declaring them artificial because they inhibit the realization of this demand.

The notion of limit is also connected with that of diversity. In fact, they mutually imply and support one another. Limits serve as the borders of things that are different. There is no difference without limits, without lines of demarcation. Otherwise everything flows into the same and becomes undifferentiated, including the river.

We therefore must question why every limit, every assertion of a difference, is today regarded as *discrimination*. To discriminate originally meant *to distinguish*. But the term today has acquired a pejorative connotation: to distinguish is itself immoral. Or at least, to distinguish appears to be connected with injustice, because when it is connected with discrimination one thinks that something that is owed a person (or act or thing) is being withheld. And today, we believe that everything is owed everything. This explains certain verbal transitions and transformations. "Illegal" becomes "undocumented." In other words, the person is not described by the limit—the law—he violated but by the purported injustice he suffered. This is because to erect a barrier, to define a distinction, between those who have official documents and those who do not is equivalent to unjust discrimination.

Taking this a step further, some maintain that it is discriminatory to refuse citizenship to foreigners living in the country. And the debate over Turkey's admission to the European Union follows the same logic. After Valéry Giscard d'Estaing, the former French president, made comments doubting Turkey's suitability for admission, he was immediately denounced for "close-minded 'identitarianism,'"[4] even "Christian fundamentalism" reminiscent of "medieval scholasticism"![5] Turkey's ambassador to Brussels expressed the thought of many Europeans when he replied: "In our view the European Union is not a closed club, fearful of opening itself to diversity-in-unity."[6] Thus, to demand limits that would make the EU a definable entity is equivalent to rejecting "the Other." This is based on the thought that in order to accept the other one must deny differences. The contrary, however, is true.

To accept the other is to accept him with his differences, not to want to simply identify him with oneself. To do the latter is to suppress him as another. To be sure, we may have great, even insurmountable, difficulties in accepting the other as other. We thus are tempted to make him like us, so as to accept him. But that is no longer to accept him as the other. He has ceased to exist.

Limits render otherness possible, otherness justifies limits.

Contemporary European universalism is based on two connected presuppositions. We are convinced of the superiority of the culture of human rights, yet we do not want to disdain other peoples. In order not to do so, we abolish—at least symbolically—the limits between us and them. We regard them as if they have already agreed to adopt the doctrine of human rights, or will do so tomorrow. If they differ from us, it is only provisionally. There is no space in which to display the differences that separate us because those differences are destined to fade away. Merely pointing them out can retard their disappearance.

As it happens, I agree with the premises of European universalism. The culture of human rights is the best for all humanity, and one must not disdain the peoples who do not adopt that culture. But the conclusion drawn from these premises, that one must therefore abolish the limits and differences between us and others, can have no positive result. If we truly respect foreign peoples, we must recognize them in their differences. And if we are convinced of the superiority of our values, we must attempt to persuade them. In fact, one can only persuade "the other as such," with his differences. As long as one does not succeed, one must tolerate him. In fact, I believe that the respect owed other peoples must be an essential part of the defense of—the apologia for—our convictions. It is that defense's sine qua non. This is why limits between cultures are not discriminatory but rather are the guarantors of dignity.

CHAPTER 10

CONTEXT AND BEING SITUATED IN THE PARTICULAR

A SINGLE, DEFINITIVE universal answer to the enigma of human existence does not exist. The human hope for it appears—imperfectly and awkwardly—in and through particular cultures. Just as each individual human being exists as a body and spirit inhabiting space and time, so are responses to the human enigma embodied in particular cultures. We cannot exist either individually or collectively without this "incarnation." For us, to be is to be determined. For us, the response to the "tragic" questions of existence can only be mediated by cultural answers. And these answers are always particular, inadequate, truncated. The necessity of incarnation and the need for mediation define us.

Only animals and God are indeterminate. Animals because they lack culture, the God of monotheism because the least definition would reduce him. But man cannot exist without determinations. This is because he does not have direct access to the truth. Unlike the animals who do not even think about truth, man does not live outside—short of—its threshold. Unlike the God of the Scriptures, he is not identical with truth. He exists in endless search for the truth of his existence. He therefore has ceaselessly to interrogate and interpret, and he has to identify himself with these interpretations. This is why there is no purely "cosmopolitan" human being. Each of us, it is true, can feel himself to be a citizen of the world by way of solidarity with all mankind, who likewise experience the "tragic" character of existence on earth. But none of us really exists except as identified first of all with a particular culture.

Between each particular culture and an eventual *culture of humanity*—which would presuppose a world government—yawns the gap that Bergson described between the *closed* and the *open*. The difference between the two is qualitative: "From the closed to the open society, from the city to humanity, one will never progress via mere enlargement. They do not belong to the same genus. The open society in principle would embrace all humanity. A dream of special souls, it realizes something of itself in the creations which effect a more or less profound transformation in man, allowing him to overcome difficulties that until then he could not. But after each one, the momentarily open circle closes."[1]

Why could we not progress step-by-step from the closed to the open, from particular cultures to a world state? Because we are immediately, straightforwardly specified by inscription in the particular; only the particular *exists*. We do not become aware of ourselves except *before others*. We cannot be recognized except *by others*. Whether individuals, groups, or cultures, we do not define ourselves except by comparison and contrast. Only diversity guarantees us determinate existence, which is existence *tout court*.

The necessity of identification, which is the condition of all real and recognizable existence, requires location in a specific time and in a specific place. Marc Augé has shown how late modernity deprives man of specificity of time by its desire to overcome history and of specificity of place by means of "globalized" space and the multiplication of anonymous, meaningless spaces.[2] Every particular culture, on the other hand, belongs to the world via geographical and historical particularities. It depends on its own particular circumstances and situations. It is defined by the specific space it occupies.

In May 1948 the former American pilot Garry Davis tore up his American passport before the U.S. embassy in Paris. By this gesture he did not simply reject his connection with his country but with any country whatsoever. He presented himself as "the first world citizen." In various ways (including staged media events) he demanded the establishment of a world government specifically tasked to prevent all wars. Albert Camus and other famous writers defended him.[3] In the same spirit, today Giorgio Agamben proposes the replacement of the citizen with the refugee: "The refugee will become at once the symbolic and real face of a transnational politics to come."[4] We see here the same desire to suppress particular identities and thus the true figure of man, with his necessarily specific determinations. If we were all refugees there would no longer be any national or partisan disputes.

I understand that one can become tired of one's particularity, as one sometimes gets tired of one's family. Sometimes one has no hope of finding a remedy that is better than the disease. In fact, to reject inscription in a particular world is a natural human attitude. Man's world always limits him, and sometimes it suffocates him. He dreams of escaping from all particularities while remaining himself. This dream is further elaborated by all the internationalisms. It is the very notion of belonging, of particular identities, that is called into question. Men are called to identify themselves essentially only with some universal culture. They should view as juvenile, as passé, their particular identities, and they should subordinate them to mature, global affiliations. And if there is a contradiction between these two sets of identifications and affiliations, the former must go.

World government represents the idea that men can find the essentials of their identity in humanity at large. The Marxists thought that the national question was merely a bourgeois matter. The bourgeoisie was still attached to particularities, to particular identities; it therefore was exclusive. But around 1920 the idea of a world workers' revolution gave way to the defense of the Soviet state as "the *homeland* of socialism." Communists soon observed that even the proletariat, the class that in theory was most open to the universal because it was deprived of everything, only wanted to be integrated into society under specific conditions. They wanted to become a distinct class, "workers" organized as such, not the "nothings" that the theoreticians decreed. Trade-unionism was one of Lenin's nightmares. The workers also remained nationalistic—that is, patriotic. Those who fought Hitler at Stalingrad fought for mother Russia, for Russian soil much more than for a universal ideology.

The identification of the singular human being with a universal culture therefore would be equivalent to lessening him, perhaps even to destroying him. One must not denigrate particular identities, because man does not realize his humanity except via inscription in a particular world. Every human being is a child of a place and a time. This is not an untoward fate but rather a necessity as demanding as that which commands him to exit his mother's womb in order to live in the world. Unlike animals, we are born twice. The unformed human who appears at biological birth must still become humanized. This only occurs through the mediation of a culture, one that is inscribed in space and time. We learn to speak by learning a particular language, for example. We learn to respect others thanks to a particular morality, to live together in a particular society's ethos or sheltering atmosphere. The universal is our horizon, but the particular is our dwelling—our hearth, even. We can never wholly get away from it even if we can put some distance between us and it, even if we can push back its limits from time to time.

A universal culture would necessarily be an abstract one. But men can only live in the concrete. Not only can men not live in the universal, they cannot even define it exactly. They can only aspire to it while imperfectly sketching its image.

The universal can never replace the particular, or even be properly compared with it. They do not exist in the same spheres, since the universal as such can never be concretized or particularized. Everything that occurs in existence is necessarily particular.

Some thinkers, however, would have us believe that cosmopolitan citizenship—world citizenship—is the soul of citizenship, and that it is an enrichment of the soul. They would have us believe that to be a citizen of a particular country is a misfortune, that it is to be a defective human being. Such a citizen, however, is both healthy and imperfect. That is, he is endowed with what I call "élan" and the possibility of self-transcendence.

The desire for the coming of world citizenship inspires each of the various internationalist ideologies. It is always a question of dis-incarnating humanity, of detaching man from his territorial and temporal roots, of making him abstract, of saturating him with indetermination. Marc Augé describes the "deterritorialized" human being living in supermarkets, airports, and parking lots, "communicating" with the entire world but not really knowing his cubicle partner.[5] In this way, the existential abstraction desired by Marxists has been realized in a certain manner by postmodernity. The multiplication of "abstract spaces" is a sign of the hoped for dis-incarnation of men, which will liberate them from particularity. This is regarded as freedom. Wanting to escape the tyranny of the particular—after all, we do not choose these particulars—we seek to install ourselves directly in the universal.

But if we *can* try to render the particular more habitable, and even attempt to surpass it, we cannot really live in the universal. When international agencies take responsibility for expatriated peoples, all they can really do is keep them from being killed or from dying; they cannot make them belong. It is jarring that Garry Davis became a hero to certain intellectuals at the very time when millions of human beings wandered desperately from place to place, having lost their countries in the aftermath of the Second World War. They sought, unsuccessfully, to breathe familiar air.

There is no universal space—the global village is at best a metaphor. Nor is there a universal time, since we live at no other time than our own. That is why it is rather pretentious and tendentious to judge history. We can try to understand the past, but judging it is another matter. We certainly cannot condescend to it from above by virtue of a universal perspective that we do not possess.

International justice is de-localized, de-temporalized. Where then will the universal law it proclaims be renewed, debated, qualified, or amended? In fact, international justice merely lives an artificial life among a small coterie of cosmopolitan intellectuals. But can one judge real human beings who committed crimes in particular places and times, in particular circumstances, with laws written in Heaven? To want to *realize* the universal, to grant it real existence, to establish it as a policy and a tribunal—this is to dis-incarnate humanity, to compel it to live in abstract kingdoms.

Man's inscription in space and time makes possible, even necessary, all sorts of acts, including the most monstrous. But to deprive an act of its context is to abandon all hope of understanding it, much less of judging it rightly. The crimes that international justice reserves for itself, however, are by definition outside any spatial context, while past crimes judged by national tribunals long after their occurrence are outside any temporal context. A Western tribunal judges Rwandan criminals without situating them in their history, their customs, their culture. International justice judges criminals according to the most "advanced" moral criteria, which can be light years removed from the morality espoused by the accused. Not to take this into account is itself an injustice.

These crimes are considered baseless, so abominable that nothing can explain them.[6] In speaking that way, the fear is expressed that putting them in their context might affect the proceedings, that there might be mitigating circumstances to what is held to be an absolute crime and therefore totally incomprehensible, totally inexcusable. The crimes of the Vichy regime were similarly judged outside of any context: they were characterized simply as metaphysical monstrosities.

In true judgment, in judgment that is just, we do not only judge an act. The act is always performed by a person who is more than—who even transcends—the act. Nor do we judge the person in his entirety, because no one can comprehend (much less judge) him in his entirety. God alone can do that. What we can do is to judge the act of this person acting in this situation.

If it is essential that a man always be judged in his circumstances, it is because he is a person, which means that he is not reducible to his action.

Every judgment therefore involves a paradox. On one hand, it is necessary for the applicable norm to be universal (at least vis-à-vis a particular society). On the other hand, the judgment must take into account the person's particular situation. We know, for example, that a murder is a murder. But we also have to acknowledge that a premeditated killing motivated by hatred is worse than an unpremeditated one committed in a fit of anger.

In international justice, neither the cultural nor the purely personal circumstances of the criminal's situation are taken into account. His cultural situation does not count because the crime he is alleged to have committed is defined by a universal natural or moral law—defined by the West—and not by any positive law. His personal situation does not count because having confronted and been horrified by National Socialism, we have established the category of metaphysical crime. This involves the affirmation of incarnations of absolute evil on earth, separated neatly into categories of innocent and guilty, victims and criminals, good and evil: two irreducible groups. This Manicheanism compels us to treat the criminal as a demon rather than as a human being. Satan is precisely the one who embodies the crime that transcends all particulars. He *is* crime.

One cannot seriously believe, however, that there are crimes devoid of all reasons and circumstances. No man—even the worse masochistic torturer—acts outside of a context. Otherwise, he really would be the Devil in person. The inescapability of context means that no man is a demon.

On the other hand, justice meted out in the name of a universal law in order to punish absolute evil is the work of angels. Here below it takes place in a very human context. Its indignations and its accusations are quite selective. In this way (and others) it is rooted in a particular culture—which is very understandable—but it is so rooted contrary to its own claims.

CHAPTER 11

CAN ONE SIMPLY TRANSFORM NATURAL LAW INTO POSITIVE LAW?

AS WE HAVE noted, late modernity marks the end of legal positivism. Westerners have regained an awareness of the existence of another law, one that transcends the positive laws of states, which they had thought were the only ones in the world. International law wants to make this overarching law itself positive. The consequences however are not positive, or even harmless.

First of all, what *is* the law before which the positivism of the past two centuries is now giving way? If contemporary international law now punishes those who wrongly obeyed certain positive laws, in the name of exactly what law does it do so?

Antigone first answered this question. She opposed Creon by appealing to "the unwritten and unshakeable laws of the gods, those which are not from today or even yesterday but are in place from all time; no one can say when they first appeared."[1] Thus is it in the name of *divine* laws and not written ones that she dared to rise up against the positive commands of human authority.[2] But since divine laws have disappeared from our civilizational memory, international law today bases itself upon universal laws found in the bosom of humanity itself, woven into mankind's heart. Beginning with Nuremberg, writes Tzvetan Todorov, "international tribunals became plausible embodiments of universal justice."[3]

Is this a resurgence of natural law? Natural law expresses an idea of some immutable Justice, an idea written on the heart of man and especially present in the most pure consciences. It is by definition, however, rather imprecise. As an idea, it is prompted by insight or supported by indignation and revolt. And it is invoked only when needed to replace the errors it descries. It therefore cannot really serve as the basis of a new international justice. It is more plausible to invoke human rights.

Selim Abou has correctly described human rights as lying at the intersection of natural law, which is connected to a universal morality, and positive law, which is bound up with particular cultures.[4] Human rights "express the historical awareness we have today of the exigencies of natural law which, itself, transcends history. . . . They therefore are relative to our time."[5] We cannot identify human rights with natural law because their content constantly evolves.

Abou follows the tradition established by Suarez. In his *De legibus*, Suarez distinguished natural law from the law of nations. The former is characterized by objective universality, the latter by a general subjective agreement. The natural law therefore is inalterable, while the law of nations changes and evolves during the course of history.

International law derives from the law of nations in the sense that it bases its principles of justice on the most powerful "world opinion" of the times—a century ago, today's commonly agreed upon charges against Milosevic would have been impossible. Because it must pronounce on concrete cases and render particular, even precise, judgments, contemporary international law can only appeal to human rights as presently understood. But it also believes that it is the direct expression and embodiment of natural law, the natural law that transcends history and escapes spatial limitations. A gap thus opens between the pretension to universality of international law and its necessarily particular character. Like all other forms of justice, this justice remains enmeshed in a particular situation while simultaneously presenting itself as absolute, transcending space and time.

The appeal to "natural law" reveals the sentiment we have of the permanent imperfection of human justice, as well as the intuition some have that there exists an immutable Justice placed at the summit of all particular justices. But the natural law is not so precisely definable by any particular group of human beings that it can form the standard for a particular court. We human beings are made in such a way that we can only grasp Justice partially, in bits and pieces and glimpses. To be sure, we can have intuitions of Injustice—especially the erring individual himself. This is what made Nuremberg legitimate, the shame that Western culture felt concerning its own actions. Natural law is a moral law, not a positive law, and only the individual can morally judge himself.

But it is as though Europeans cannot get rid of positivism except by re-creating or reenacting it at another level. They cannot imagine the *other law* that they are sure must reign over positive laws except as positive—that is, as written and prescribed but judging and punishing in a universal manner. This is because they no longer can grasp the unwritten laws found in men's hearts and in their consciences, laws their predecessors and ancestors recognized. Therefore, proponents of international justice want to erect natural law into positive law.[6] They claim to fix this law, inscribe it in stone, and appoint themselves as its sole possessors and guardians.

But can a tribunal claiming to judge solely in the name of the natural law really exist? A court that would be the pure and direct expression of Antigone?

Unwritten law by definition is without a text, and the effort to "textualize" it always leads to one form or another of clerical tyranny. It cannot be written down by a court because it is impossible to concretely define a norm that by definition is universal and atemporal.

At once universal and abstract, natural law does not allow itself to be laid down in statutes; it cannot become positive. It belongs more to morality than to law, and hence is a matter of conscience. A community ruled by natural law would be by that very fact abstract.

If international law cannot base itself directly upon natural law, it can connect with what the Romans, and then Renaissance thinkers, called the law of nations, *jus gentium*. This law holds "that men universally agree on certain principles of justice which their common reason, reflecting upon nature, dictates."[7] The law of nations, "an offshoot derived from natural law," was developed by Suarez and Vittoria at the same time as the conceptualization of international law.[8] It is derived from a consensus or agreement between different political societies (which have different positive laws) on common norms concerning their coexistence. Political societies desirous of establishing a supranational community naturally would want to base it directly on natural law, but they cannot, because of natural law's inability to be fully realized in the world, or because of the impossibility of going from approximate descriptions to concrete norms. They therefore must content themselves with a substitute, the law of nations, which is at once real and articulable, but temporal and subject to the acceptance of the parties involved. For Suarez, "natural law is therefore unique and inalterable, while the law of nations is defined only by the agreement of the greatest number at any given time, and is subject to change and variation."[9]

We therefore must connect human rights to the law of nations. It is incorrect to define human rights as an expression of natural law, as Blandine Kriegel, for example, does: "What has progressed, what marks an unquestionable advance, is the recognition of the universal character of human rights whose content, one must say, is entirely commonplace: equality, security, liberty, property—these are nothing else but the most common prescriptions of the most widespread morality, which one finds not only in all the great civilizations but in all human societies."[10] One, however, has to twist the meaning of words to maintain that equality, liberty and property are values found in all cultures. . . . And when we include in human rights property rights, the autonomy of women, respect for homosexuals, or the abolition of the death penalty, it is clear that none of these norms finds expression in all human societies. Human rights are closer to the law of nations, the ensemble of principles recognized by a large number of societies at a given time. They thus express where humanity is in its laborious search for the always unattainable natural law. But one of the errors of our time is to confuse natural law with the law of nations.

To derive international law from the law of nations and not from natural law would not deprive it of legitimacy but would transform its pretensions. Once it was aware that its norms are interpretations and not tablets descended from on High, international law would lose the certitude of its complete and total objectivity. Forced to obtain a consensus, it would have to respect the societies that do not recognize its norms, and it would have to seek to persuade rather than to compel them. Knowing the provisional character of these norms, it would consider itself to be the particular depository of a historically conditioned conviction and not God the Father in person.

If there must be an ultimate norm or authority, it can only be the individual conscience, and this requirement entails that international law cannot be the final authority, the single repository of unquestionable universal laws. In fact, international law wars with individual conscience, to the point that each wants to get rid of the other. This is the heart of the matter, its central point.

What historically happens when a political authority, master of the positive law, exercises its powers abusively, criminally? A few consciences endowed with discernment and courage find themselves capable of naming the crime (which is not always simple or easy). Then they rise up against the offending authority, assuming the risks of combat, with victory doubtful at best. This is the story of Antigone. In the twentieth century, it is the story of the Sakharovs and the Solzhenitsyns, or of the two young German students, Sophie and Hans Scholl, who belonged to the anti-Nazi group White Rose. They barely had time to distribute a few thousand tracts before being discovered and executed.[11]

It is precisely in this taut and tragic battle that international law interferes. By pursuing criminals or their accomplices who obeyed the positive law of their state, it frontally attacks the freedom and consciences of individuals in situations of the utmost complexity—that is, when freedom of judgment is most needed. It pretends to do the work of which conscience has shown itself incapable.

But isn't Antigone's path, as steep and craggy as it is, that through which exceptional consciences always pass? And can one condemn another person for not being a hero? That is exactly what is being done. When positive law is directed against the human beings it claims to serve, the usual path is that of compliance and turning a blind eye. Must one criminalize all accomplices with dull consciences? We always can admire Antigone or the very young Sophie Scholl and their emulators. They had that exceptional judgment and courage which are necessary to take on the power of positive law, and thus they sacrificed their lives. But can we punish those who do not follow Antigone? Hannah Arendt wrote the following, with a skepticism or doubt in her voice that led to her banishment from the intellectual community: "We demand that a human being should be able to distinguish good from evil even when he or she only has her own judgment for guide, and when this judgment finds itself in contradiction with the unanimous opinion of its environment."[12] A court that pursues this particular sort of criminal really punishes nothing other than individual conscience in its most difficult moments, when it must decide in solitude. The grandeur of the human person resides in these demanding and dramatic situations when it must debate alone with itself in the face of the enigmas of good and evil. If after such exceptional situations it then has to answer to a man-made institution, isn't it radically demeaned, almost annihilated?

The tribunal that claims to judge consciences acting in such extreme situations indicates by that very fact that individual conscience cannot rise against it. It is the judge, while the individual conscience has lost the freedom to judge power. This particular positive law—raised up above all others—thus expresses and indicates the limit on acceptable dissent before human law. To establish a tribunal to judge the moral conscience is to abolish the latter. We have been here before. The Inquisition was terroristic in its basic principle, which was to establish a tribunal of, and for, morality.

In its order, however, individual conscience is supreme or it does not exist. It is conscience that must be able to appeal to a superior law if the laws of man fall short. Who will judge international law? To what, or whom, will one appeal against it if it is deemed to represent the ultimate earthly norm, especially at a time when Heaven is believed to be closed? It really is great hubris to believe that a human law or institution could be so universal and so perfect that no one confronted by it could appeal to a higher law. The partisans of international law have not banished fallibility, the necessarily partial character of every human law, including their own. If something like natural law exits it is not formulable by human words, at least not clearly enough to serve penal justice. We can only perceive its emanations, in glimmers and bits and pieces. On the other hand, individual conscience represents the most complex and the most acute organ for discernment. It is precisely the fallibility of our laws and decisions that confers special importance on the freedom of conscience. Infallibility and conscience are mutually exclusive. Neither the Inquisition nor the totalitarian states would have countenanced Antigone. Nor does international law.

We cannot *institutionalize* the revolts of conscience.

CHAPTER 12

WORLD GOVERNMENT OR THE END OF POLITICS

WITH INTERNATIONAL LAW come institutions endowed with the authority to take citizens away from the protection and authority of their states. States lose their monopoly of command and judgment. One can compare this development with the process that led governments to deprive fathers of certain kinds of authority at the end of the fourth century, under the influence of the church. The paterfamilias of the Roman tradition had the power of life and death over his children. Taking away his sovereign authority was motivated by a desire to protect individuals from arbitrary personal authority.

The Le Chapelier law of 1791 that suppressed intermediate institutions, whether corporate or not, followed the same logic. It sought to remove individuals from the arbitrary and abusive authority of local or inferior powers by placing them under the direct protection of the state. With the sovereign authority of international law it is now this higher echelon of authority that finds itself dispossessed as a dangerous power by a still higher authority.

In each case, the individual finds himself confronting a higher and more remote power, with this distance believed to guarantee objectivity by avoiding the temptations that lead to arbitrariness. With international law, an additional step in that direction is taken. It is presented as the last step. Jürgen Habermas sums up the thinking as follows: "The key to cosmopolitan law resides in the fact that it concerns the status of subjects of individual rights, not merely collective subjects, thereby founding a direct connection with the association of free and equal cosmopolitans."[1]

The threat that international law so conceived poses to states radically transforms the nature of political societies (in addition to the inconvenience that "war crimes" and "crimes against humanity" are floating categories whose definition is left to individual determination). A government has the task of consolidating and guaranteeing the existence of a particular common world, one founded on a culture, on a common history and a shared destiny. It does not establish the common world; rather, it reinforces it in its own desire to exist and persevere. Government protects its continuation. In order to do so, common purposes have to be defined, decisions have to be made, and consequent actions have to be performed. The actions can go so far as, and include, the use of force, if necessary. Since it aims to protect a particularity and therefore finds itself within a pluralistic world, political power only exists in the distinction between "same and other." At the extreme, this means "friend-enemy."* One cannot deprive government of the means of affirming this distinctiveness without destroying this specificity. If war exists, it is not because men do not love justice enough, but because they only can grasp *particular* justices.

However, if *any* government can be called into question for using force in a way others judge illicit or unworthy, then the necessary consequence is that political authority itself—the final institution of command, the final declarer of the community's ends—is undermined. Henceforth, the criterion of the legitimacy of a government resides in the morality of its conduct, a morality whose interpretation depends on external, foreign

* Delsol alludes to the famous distinction, inherent in "the political as such," made by the German jurist and political theologian Carl Schmitt (1888–1985).

institutions and agencies largely beholden to "world opinion." This is a far cry from the idea that legitimacy derives from free and fair elections, or even from the generally recognized fact that it is legitimate.

In the new situation, a political leader cannot use force without fearing that it will be treated as a crime, and he as a criminal. Nor is there any comfort in the laws and statutes supposedly governing the respective judgments. The categories named in the Treaty of Rome are so broad that one has to ask if their aim is to outlaw war itself. The treaty states, for example, that "the fact of killing or wounding *by treacherous means* individuals belonging to the enemy nation or army" can be considered a war crime (italics added). Is this an instance of humanizing war or of wanting to suppress it? If any act of war can be considered a crime, the truth is that the goal is to end the use of force by states. But to deny politics the legitimate possibility of using force is to deconstruct particular political community, to take away from government its most determinative power.

As in other areas, in the domain of social organization politics corresponds to a feeling of uncertainty in the face of the questions of human existence. In speaking of "politics" I do not mean "government," exactly. Government means the authority to command, which can be more or less complex, and which all peoples have and employ. Politics refers to a distinctive form of activity tied to a specific form of government. The activity was born in Greece and from there it has spread throughout the Western world.

Politics in this sense—*stricto sensu*, if you will—presupposes that it is impossible to arrive at a sole certain and objective answer to the problem of the common good. Instead, it seeks to integrate a plurality, a variety, of thoughts and proposals; it holds any and all discourse about the common good to be a matter of opinion, not certain knowledge or science. In the words of Aristotle, this kind of government aims to make human diversity a harmony, not a total unity.

In this sense, a world government could exist but not world politics. This is because politics, by presupposing uncertainty concerning the definition of the common good, is conditioned by the existence of interior and exterior contradictions, by differences recognized as such.

In the international arena the diversity of governments and ways of governing corresponds to the different ways of understanding human existence and hence human happiness, which is the common goal of human beings but incapable of a common definition. True, the majority of past and present governments in the world assumed that their definition of the common good was the best and did not allow a diversity of views in their midst. Most governments of which we are aware are despotic, in the sense that a single vision of the common good is imposed as a matter of knowledge, of certainty. The specifically Western form of *politics*, which admits a plurality of views of the common good and lets them govern in turn, remains the exception in world history.

That is why there would be no qualitative gap or break between a particular despotic government and a universal world government, which would only be the former's extension to the entirety of humanity. Each time in history that a government wanted to achieve world empire—admittedly in a "world" much smaller than today—it was a despotism that wanted to extend its field of action but not change its intrinsic nature. It would be a quite different change if a *political* government tried to become a world government. Then it would have to qualitatively change and become despotic rather than political. This is because, as we said, politics presupposes the acceptance of diversity within and without. And uncertain of the answer to give to human enigmas, it allows and lives by debate between different answers. If a political government claimed to impose its idea of the common good on the entire world, it would cease to be political. Liberty, itself connected to the uncertainty of answers, belongs consubstantially to politics. As Ulrich Beck said, the cosmopolitan regime "does not directly abolish democracy, but little by little suffocates it under the imperceptible narrowing of understanding, and renders it superfluous. . . . Democracy becomes the religion of the past. . . . It is the dead god of the First Modernity."[2] International law and world government are thus incompatible with democracy.

World government would not only signify the end of politics in the strict sense, as government combined with freedom for different points of view, but also of politics *lato sensu*, as government endowed with the monopoly of legitimate force.

The project of establishing world institutions and government agencies comes from the will to confront political forces that have become blind, arbitrary, or terroristic. These institutions would compel governments to give an account of the use of force inside their own borders. At the same time, they would inhibit or stop them from conducting war outside their borders, or at least punish them if they were to act in such a way. The monopoly of legitimate force is therefore withdrawn from particular governments and granted to international institutions and eventually world government. No particular government will be sheltered from being prosecuted for the acts of force that it may undertake, whenever the world institution judges it to be unjustified. Moreover, since the world tribunal would not content itself with judging criminal governments but also those individuals who obeyed purportedly criminal orders—after all, it presumes to judge all positive laws and all political conduct in the name of absolute morality—we would see the emergence of a *world moral authority* operating against particular—in fact, any and all—politics. For if from now on no one can seek and find shelter under any positive law (which is what international law demands), if each one of us is personally responsible to this tribunal for his actions, what value can any national purpose have, in the name of which governments and citizens decide, and in the name of which they employ force? And how will international law distinguish between *acceptable* political *force* and the political *violence* that is *intolerable* and therefore punishable?

As we said, in proclaiming itself competent to morally judge every political action, the tribunal aims to establish a world moral order, one designed to substitute for politics. Every political decision properly speaking is only allowed on the condition that world government and its agencies have the final word. Given the vagueness, uncertainty, and fluctuation connected with the definition of "intolerable violence," no government would be able to employ force without fearing an accusation. In such a situation, one could hardly call these governments.

If this substitution really did effect the ending of war and the use of arbitrary force, one might applaud it. But this would not be the case, for a cogent reason: the institutions of world government would remain composed of humans responding to questions that always bear their human mark. War would not be suppressed. Rather, it would be the world government that would define "just wars" and decree that certain acts of violence are legitimate because of its "objective" knowledge of the common good.

In other words, this substitution, while designed to replace the violence and arbitrariness of political power, would reestablish both at a higher level—but now in the hands of a single authority. Thus, the idea of world government expresses the secret dream of Western Europe since at least the twentieth century, the dream of replacing politics. But in this idea politics reappears, and in a more disquieting way because of its monopolistic character.

We human beings do not have the means to suppress politics understood as power capable of arbitrariness. We can only mitigate its perversions by means of comparisons—that is, by diversity.

CHAPTER 13

THE PROCESS AND THE ÉLAN

INTERNATIONAL JUSTICE AND world government are viewed by contemporary minds as consequences of a *process*. They are an advancement to be accomplished in time, during human history. Theory as well as practice express this way of looking at things. When Albert Camus in the aftermath of World War II invoked the necessity of a world government, he spoke of "managing" a problem, of finding a "solution."[1] The current elaboration of international law obeys the same imperative. It is admitted that this form of justice can appear unjust because today it is in a transition period. The process is at work, but it is as yet incomplete. Everything happens as though the international community were conquering a territory: you begin where you can. It is even admitted that the less-than-optimal or universal judgments occurring now would be shocking, even revolting, if they occurred in a particular society. But one can explain and justify them because they are inscribed in an inevitable process. And this process makes success not merely possible, but guaranteed.

But if one views this aspiration for international law and justice in the context of its original founding convictions and postulates, one discovers that by this very expectation of success it betrays its own presuppositions, or at least misunderstands them.

The realization of universal justice and world government would represent the completion or realization of the Stoic and Pauline idea of the unity of the human race. The Stoics and Saint Paul, however, affirmed this unity in the ontological order, not the political order. To say that the human race is *one* is to say that all human beings are equally worthy and have equal dignity. It does not mean that we must abolish cultural borders. Human beings are equally worthy not in the expectation that their diverse laws will be changed or abolished but *despite* the diversity of their laws.

The aspiration for international law and justice, and hence world government, cannot be realized except via a category mistake, the confusion of the political with the ontological. Contemporary European culture does not want to abandon the Pauline idea of the unity of the human race, but it does want to detach it from its underlying ontology. The idea is therefore radicalized by the exorbitant desire for its complete realization in the historical world.

Stoic cosmopolitanism and later the Catholic (or universal) Church aimed at invoking, but with appropriate qualifications, human unity. But they knew that such unity was impractical—unattainable—in this world. These invocations were not signs of a process, much less a necessary one, but of élans, moments of elevation and inspiration that indicate humanity's aspirations. Christians in particular knew that concrete unity would destroy rather than advance humanity because humanity is composed of singular individuals and groups from which it derives its very life. Men and women were not the agents of a unifying process advancing toward completion, but common participants in a paradox that defined them: they shared in singularity *and* in the aspiration for unity. Awareness of "the better" will always be ahead of its concrete realization, because the two are separated and joined, or mediated, by liberty. Christ himself neither established nor conquered a temporal kingdom in order to establish the kingdom of justice and righteousness. Mohammed reproached him for this, and when Islamic governments establish constitutions devoted to "imposing the good and forbidding evil," they are compelled to banish liberty.

The Christian response to the story of Babel is Pentecost. Then, in a moment of grace that transcends history, the disciples were granted a perfect agreement that rose above particular languages. The true consequence of the Stoic and Pauline postulate is not a political search for the concrete unity of the various moralities and justices of humanity. It is a quest for communion by beings who acknowledge their various particularities. This spiritual postulate requires a spiritual response. A world government would only be a grotesque—and no doubt violent—caricature of the Catholic Church and of Stoic cosmopolitanism.

In the contemporary version of the unity of the human race, that unity is sapped of its true spirit, which is *hope*. It ceases being hopeful when it becomes a process of construction, the expectation of a result. This denaturing belongs to the mode of thought that only sees the alternatives of utopian dreams and projects and finished products. It does not know, or it ignores, the option of *hope*, of walking on an indefinite path toward the good. In this way, advocates of international law and world government are the heirs of the ideologues of the twentieth century. They aimed to immanentize a spiritual good. They wanted to give it concrete form and content, to make it visible and real. The unity of the human race became an idol to fashion rather than an ideal that one has to pursue without respite. The idolater is the one who confuses categories. And he confuses them because he has forgotten that he is a human being, in the Latin sense of *humus*: soil, earth, ground.

On the other hand, a culture that does not seek unity, that is satisfied with its particularity and extols it, will collapse upon itself. The Lama Jigné Rinpoché defined *nirvana* in the Buddhist tradition in this way: Unlike what Westerners believe (who in this sense follow Hinduism rather than Buddhism), nirvana is not a dissolution of the self but its effacement as an ego. Put another way, it is the emergence of the individual spirit insofar as it aspires to universality. The "awakened" spirit finds itself loosened from the particularities that seem to define it entirely and imprison it in the particular and partial. "It experiences its essential nature, its ultimate nature, synonymous with total openness and total clarity."[2] But is this "awakening" possible? Can man think of himself outside of the particularities upon which his existence is based? (A bit later we will look at a certain view of the European hero that approaches this idea. We also will see the consequences one can draw from this view.)

It follows that the aspiration to escape from particularity characterizes man as a moral being. Julien Freund rightly remarked that "the cosmopolitan, since the Stoics, has always had a moral significance."[3] The original human instinct, our nature in its original "nakedness," first of all seeks the particular and only loves the near, the known, the recognizable, the familial, the similar. Interest in the far-off and the different arises out of effort and from elevation of the soul. Love for all mankind follows from charity in the biblical sense and requires a certain self-overcoming, going beyond the warm closed circle of reassuring proximity. It forswears the satisfactions of always encountering the same.

Therefore, the establishment of a world society would require universal solidarity, which would overcome particular egoisms. This is a practical moral task demanding virtues, not a political or technical one pertaining to institutions (even if they can play roles as means). But as with every moral task, it lives in the hope that nourishes it rather than in the expectation of its necessary success.[4]

Montesquieu penned the following famous epigram: "If I knew something was useful to me but prejudicial to my family I would banish it from my mind. If I knew something was useful to my family but was not to my country, I would seek to forget about it. If I knew something was useful to my country but prejudicial to Europe and to mankind, I would consider it a crime."[5] But his contemporary Hume on the other hand wrote: "Consanguinity produces the strongest bond of which the human mind is capable. . . . Consanguinity [however] is not the only one to have this effect; every other relation without exception produces it equally. We love our fellow countrymen, our neighbors, people of the same trade or profession or even the same name as us."[6] Today, moral indignation arises in response to anything resembling Hume's thought, while Montesquieu's seems to be the sole moral truth. Today, we are to believe that the love of humanity is normal (in both senses of the term), while the love of the particular is ignoble. But both are human. Love of the particular is natural, and the natural cannot be denigrated: it exists, and it belongs to life. Because of this it merits consideration, as do other aspects of life.

When the aspiration for the universal and for unity takes the form of a process of fabrication, it necessarily entails the abhorrence of particularities. They have to be expunged in order for the desired unity to occur in the here-and-now. There is therefore a great difference between the hero of the universal and the cosmopolitan ideologue who hates all particularities. The hero advances with great hope toward the universal, but he does not forget or leave behind any of the mediations that constitute men. One troubling consequence of the multiplication of ideologues is that peoples have responded by defending their scorned particularities in a way that rejects the universal entirely. They are deceived by the false advocates of false universals.

Suarez concluded from his reflections on international relations that a community of nations represents at once a hope, a path, and an endeavor.[7] For Kant, a universal community is a never-attained ideal, permanently pursued but never attained or realized. The élan for the universal, like the ethical élan, cannot be translated politically. This is because men are defined by the particularities imposed by the plurality of cultural worlds. The élan for the universal *could* be translated politically, but then it would destroy its own raison d'être, the very legitimacy and morality of its spirit, because it immediately would produce despotism. Why? Because morality is the interiority of a free conscience.[8] To deny that there is a real, concrete process of construction leading to the universal society is not the same thing as denying the élan toward the universal.

This élan in fact represents humanity's vocation as it liberates itself from tribal particularism.[9] But one must locate, or relocate, the élan in its proper order and understand its true nature. This means accepting its intrinsically unrealizable character. One has to inscribe—that is, particularize—it in space and time. One has to accept its unforeseeable risks, costs, and conditions, since it operates only in freedom.

CHAPTER 14

CONQUEST VERSUS QUEST

THE IMPOSSIBILITY OF being fully realized makes international justice a matter of quest rather than conquest. It is closer to the Holy Grail than the Golden Fleece.

The object of "conquest" is attainable. One conquers a territory or attains a throne. Jason seized the Golden Fleece and returned to Greece with it in order to give it to King Peleus.

A "quest," in contrast, is an uninterrupted search for an object that is at once desirable and unattainable. The knights of the Round Table sought the Holy Grail. But in the end they did not find it (with one exception).

What does this essential difference between a successful undertaking, no matter how demanding and trying, and the equally demanding search for something one knows one never will possess mean? What does it mean to enter a race without a finish line?

Conquest's stage is the closed world, an immanent world in which everything exists on a human scale, even the gods. All desirable objects find their home here. I would even say that they do not move. To possess an object, one merely has to seek it, albeit with an effort commensurate to its value. The stage for a quest, conversely, is an open world, one that has unknown aspects and dimensions. This openness does not necessarily entail an opening to transcendence. It would be too facile, or even false, to believe in a simple dichotomy: conquest's world is immanent and closed, quest's open and spiritual—or, in religious terms, to maintain that the first is polytheistic or pantheistic, the second, monotheistic, in the sense in which God dwells in another world. This is not the right contrast.

Quest's world is one in which man is never satisfied with his condition. In such a world, "fatality" makes no sense. In such a world, man always wants to rise higher, to rise above. In order to do that, he must define the object of his desire so that he can tend toward it, even if he knows that it exceeds his definition.

The voyage for the Golden Fleece is replete with perils; it is structured by a point of departure and moves toward a destination. While labyrinthine, the voyage is comprehensible. The heroes of the Argo know where they are going. By undertaking the voyage, they progress toward their desired object, which they finally see and take hold of, although not without great trouble. They then savor their acquisition.

The quest for the Grail is just that: a quest. King Arthur's companions do not know where the Grail is, nor the way to seek it. They leave the Round Table, symbol and place of friendship and quotidian happiness. They take different paths and experience what are called *adventures.* These perilous encounters, rather than bringing them closer to some exact location, bring them closer to themselves, to a knowledge of their strengths and weaknesses, to self-awareness. *Adventures,* in this sense. are less *tests* (for example, crossing a ford or a pass) than they are *ordeals* designed to reveal the truth. The Argonauts travel as a group and unite their forces in order to attain the goal that, after all, is external to them. The knights travel alone, and each is tested in his soul.

What about Sir Galahad, you ask? At the end of the quest he alone, free from sin, contemplates the Grail. But he immediately is rapt up to the heavens. He does not "survive" the vision. Contrary to a conquest, a quest does not end with possession but with a rupture in time, some completion of history. This is because it is its own end or purpose. It expresses an élan that expands and deepens humanity.

The true search for international justice is more a quest than a conquest. Its object is not a "result" that humanity can and should expect to achieve in history. Nor is it a task to be pursued in common by putting in place certain institutions or by any other means. No definite path leading to it exists. It is a hope planted in the heart of every human being who seeks the adventure of the universal.

If we employ the categories of Max Weber, the quest for universal or international justice pertains to the ethics of conviction rather than the ethics of responsibility. It is a moral calling and adventure, not a political program. It therefore is tied to "witnessing" (more anon) and patience. Each society, like an Arthurian knight, finds itself before an ordeal. As for patience: "Patience is similar to the emerald that always remains green. . . . One cannot better defeat an enemy than by patience," said the hermit to Lancelot.[1] This is why contemporary discussions, both here and abroad, asserting the necessity of eradicating tyrants and tyranny as a task required by human rights are wrong-headed. The quest for a more perfect world is asymptotic; it is an adventure that improves its seekers more than it expects a successful outcome. In fact, should international justice and law arrive in the form in which we dream, or demand, it would be the end of human history, the definitive exit from the human condition.

CHAPTER 15

PERSUASION AND WITNESSING

IT IS DOUBTLESSLY legitimate to hope for the slow emergence of an organized international community, but that community will appeal to moral values and not take shape in political institutions. Its status as universal would distinguish and separate it from politics, in which the particular reigns, diffused and structured in multiple societies. In contrast to the political, the moral can be universal. But unlike the political, morality cannot legitimately coerce. Therefore, a world community would have to use other means than political ones to have its certainties prevail. The defense of political community—in all its forms—legitimates the use of coercion, because political society represents a particular world that human beings absolutely need in order to live, think, and develop. Political society is the atmosphere without which human beings cannot breathe at all, and this atmosphere is by its nature particular.

Universal values are freely expressed norms whose realization would allow humanity to freely advance towards the summits—in a manner of speaking, to become more human. It would be false, dangerous, and useless to want morality to use the means employed by politics to apply its norms. Such a morality would then become a *moral order*, in other words, a morality gone astray that betrays its own goals by wanting to establish its reign by compulsion. International justice goes even further in this direction when it tries to combine morality and order. It becomes an inquisitorial morality.

What form should morality take, since it cannot employ either force or law? If it wants to be honest with itself, it will only use debate and counsel. Morality *diffuses* itself, it does not *impose* itself. Camus saw this very well after World War II: "In the years to come, across the five continents one will see an endless struggle between violence and preaching."[1] What is needed is "in every circumstance, to oppose example to power, preaching to domination, dialogue to insult, and simple integrity to ruse."[2]

When a moral idea wants to prevail it must indefatigably seek to convince. But not only that. It must be practiced at the same time (and place) it is being preached, in order to show that it is a matter of actions and not only words. Camus spoke of both "example" and "preaching." Montesquieu, who rejected intervention and colonialization in the name of letting people remain attached to their customs, wrote: "In general, people are very attached to their customs; to take them away violently is to make it miserable."[3] But he did not demand that each one of their laws remain untouched or unchanged. He called for change to be adapted to the developing desires and attitudes of the people. The desire for transformation comes from knowledge of other ways of behaving that are thought to be better. Progress comes from communication between peoples. "The more that peoples communicate, the easier they will change their manners, because each one is an example for the other."[4]

What the law that poses limits and constraints says differs from what the discourse of persuasion says, as well as from the silence connected with witnessing. The last two methods accept a plurality of points of view, even when they are rooted in internal certainty. He who gives witness and attempts to convince lives in the register of modesty. To be sure, he is interiorly persuaded of the rectitude of his convictions.

For example, he firmly believes that any human being is happier in a constitutional state that allows for liberty of conscience and opinion. He therefore attempts to live in accordance with that belief and to advance arguments justifying his way of life to others who live and believe differently. However, despite his own certainty he finds himself confronting, and in a certain way impotent before, the different certainties that others oppose to him when he presents himself as an example. He has to make strenuous efforts to justify his vision of the good life, even though it would be easier to simply decree the good life and impose it upon the world by law and force.

There is another difficulty that the proponents of morality with its distinctive means have to confront. Persuasion takes a long time. How many decades or even centuries will it take to convince Muslims to consider women as independent human beings endowed with the same autonomy as men? Especially if we renounce coercing them, whether by force, threat, or mockery? We cannot really believe that it will be enough merely to wave aloft the banner of human rights in order for all other cultures to fall in step with us, charmed by our tune. Around the time of the invasion of Iraq, fifty-eight American intellectuals who supported President Bush's policy wrote an open letter titled "Why We Fight" and addressed it to German and Saudi intellectuals. The latter, numbering 154, responded with a courteous but firm letter: "The American signees concentrate their attention on the necessity of separating church and state, and they see in this a universal value that ought to be adopted by every nation. We Muslims however see the relationship between religion and the state differently. . . . We believe that secularization is inappropriate to a Muslim society because it denies the members of this society the right to apply general laws to shape their lives, as well as violates their will under the pretext of protecting minorities."

He who acts in the domain of morality—and not in politics—must therefore equip himself with patience. And "patience" comes from the Latin word *pati*, which means "to suffer." One certainly suffers in seeing how the Taliban treat women. Nonetheless, this patience is required by the recognition that the remedy would be worse than the malady. One does not act morally with political means, at least not with impunity.

Simone Weil described very well the way in which impatience is a form of idolatry of the good. It inappropriately tries to transport the good into concrete life when and where it does not yet possess roots. "Idolatry comes when one desires absolute good but does not have supernatural discretion, and one does not have the patience to let things take root and sprout."[5] One idolizes the constitutional state when one wants to establish it immediately, by force if necessary, where it does not yet have roots in custom. Neither the constitutional state nor the autonomy of women is a deity to which the existential atmosphere of other peoples can be sacrificed. They are goods, but not absolutes. We cannot will the good immediately, without the mediation of time. We Europeans very slowly accomplished the transformations that we want to impose on others without any period of transition. And when we have acted precipitously, we have acted just like those we now oppose. To take one example, what the Taliban recently did to Buddhists, we did in South America in the sixteenth century. Every truly moral development requires such a passing through experiences, regrets, and sorrows. Only after a long voyage can the conscience recognize evil as such.

That the realization of world justice belongs to morality and not to politics entails other consequences. The pursuit of the good is not something to resolve simply, or even primarily, by suitably designed institutions. It is not to be systematically conducted by judicial personnel. Rather, it is called forth by the indignation of those who refuse to be satisfied with the current state of the world. These witnesses to the universal resemble the heroes Bergson talked about, those who effect the transition from a closed morality to an open one. It belongs to those "privileged souls" who see further than their contemporaries and enlarge the field of vision of moral consciousness. In themselves they "expand society's soul, . . . break the circle and bring society with them."[6] It is characteristic of these heroes to move from the closed to the open: "Privileged souls have arisen who feel they are connected with all other souls and who, instead of remaining within the limits of the group and simply adhering to the solidarity that nature established, by means of an impulse of love they turn toward all of humanity."[7] Bergson likens this élan to that of artistic creation.[8] On one hand, it is not "rational." It breaks with received thoughts and reveals a discovery, or the sudden appearance, of heretofore latent capacities in humanity. Aristotle, for example, asked whether slavery is as natural as his contemporaries believed. Las Casas argued that Indians possess a soul like us. Voltaire maintained that torture is unworthy of humanity. These awakeners of conscience enable morality to deploy itself much more surely than do institutions. The universalization of the good is not a matter of political construction but of the slow work of transmission. The heroes that Bergson talked about were moved by love (otherwise they would not have been moved by an ethical impulse). They were not moved by mere reason. That is why, said Bergson, the Stoics did not transform the world in the way that Christians did.

At this point, the objection that comes naturally to mind is the following: Persuasion and witnessing, which are as virtuous as the morality that they wish to prevail, nonetheless are unsuited to very grave situations, the ones that interest us. In the extreme case, what must be done if a foreign tyrant goes about methodically killing his people? Do we have other resources than merely casting verbal spears into the abyss? Can we—must we—simply allow things to continue? I believe that we can enter into war with such a tyrant if we believe that it is a just war. However, the meaning of "just war" is complex.

CHAPTER 16

JUST WAR AND POLITICAL DECISION

JACQUES ELLUL WROTE in August 1947: "Nuremberg was a trial in name only, because it fell into no known legal category. The crimes for which the accused were judged and punished belonged to the category of morality, not law. In fact, the tribunal denied the elementary principle of law: *nullum crimen, nulla poena, sine lege* ("without law, there is no crime, no punishment").[1]

Ellul asks: Why did the victorious democracies devote themselves to this parody of a trial? Because they wanted to distinguish themselves in an absolutely clear manner from the arbitrariness of totalitarianism. They did so, however, in a most dangerous way. They left the impression that they—the democracies—always and only use the instruments of law, never those of judgment or force. They thus created a smokescreen, deceiving public opinion into overestimating its ability to submit every political decision to law. And in this case—the punishment of Nazi criminals—they clothed an eminently political decision in the vestments of law.

Ellul does not at all deny the correctness of this punishment, but he denounces the hypocrisy of the democracies when they said: "Behold law!" He probably would have agreed with Churchill's suggestion: Hang the Nazi leaders without any further legal procedure. For Ellul, Nuremberg represents a first act of legerdemain by which *political* democracy claims to submit itself wholly to law, thus positioning itself as the polar opposite of totalitarianism. Political democracy, however, continues to be a form of politics, and as such it cannot escape from decisions and their risks.

A current of contemporary thought, particularly strong in France, Belgium, and Germany, identifies *just* war with *legal* war. In order to decrease the incidents of hostility, one must wait for the approval of the institutions that speak in the name of international law (i.e., the UN). This is the argument that these three countries gave in explanation of their criticism of the American invasion of Iraq. (This is a strange argument, given that in the case of Serbia these same countries did not wait for UN approval. That, no doubt, was a different matter.) Thus, no war is justified unless it is legalized by the organs of international law.

An act of war, however, cannot take on legal form. The "legalization of war" essentially denies war by transforming it into a police action. This approach has its difficulties. First, it puts us in the impossible situation of legally determining when a kind or level of violence is so intolerable that it legitimates force in response. This threshold is fundamentally subjective. Moreover, a situation of war is a crisis, what some thinkers have called "a limit-situation," and as such it cannot be evaluated wholly in legal terms. It demands judgment, decision . . . and conscience. Only the *normal* situation can be subject wholly to a *norm*.

Our certitude that we are witnessing an evil which absolutely must be stopped never confers on us a *right* to coerce. Such a certitude can only give us awareness of the necessity to act in order to protect and save innocents. One can even maintain that a war of humanitarian intervention is legitimate in the sense of being moved by justified indignation before gross evil. But it does not as such become *legal*. Indignation cannot be codified in positive law. It requires personal judgment.

In this case, just war begins with the following sort of reasoning: This is intolerable to me and I will not tolerate it. It is probably absolutely, not relatively, intolerable, but in any case I find it intolerable. I therefore will run the risk of getting involved in something that perhaps does not directly relate to me. However, human suffering and injustice do concern me as a human being. I therefore will intervene by force in order to stop it. In this way, entering into war does not depend on a juridical or legal mechanism but on a *political decision*.

A corollary to every decision is the uncertainty inherent in judgment and the risk of arbitrariness. Those who, on the other hand, equate just war with legally authorized war hope to rule out the inherent subjectivity of political decision by replacing it with obedience to legal rules. But this does not avoid arbitrariness; it only relocates it. As we have seen, those who pronounce in the name of international law are not incorporeal angels animated by pure love of justice. They are human beings, sometimes politicians, who *decide* that the borders between the just and the unjust must be placed *here*. The grave error of international institutions is to believe that their subjective judgments are objective. There is nothing worse than this dictation, from on high, of the norms of justice, which no one may resist. Before such pronouncements, due suspicion dims and the critical spirit sleeps. One vests a blind confidence in the UN to decide finally on the legitimacy of war. This is the same UN that allowed Libya to head its commission on human rights.

It is much better to let a particular government decide to conduct a war of intervention on the basis of its own subjective judgment, one recognized as such. It then will think that it is right, but it also can be judged and critiqued by other nations. The United States is convinced that it was right to invade Iraq. Many peoples disagree, and indignantly so. They are not wrong to say so. But the sole remedy against the arrogance of certainty is this diversity of views and opinions. In the case of international organs claiming to declare whether war is legitimate or not, there no longer is anything to say, because with them we have entered into the *illusion of objectivity*.

In the face of intolerable crimes committed outside our borders, it is better to make the decision for war than to try to take up the instrument of law. In this domain, war—even with what it contains of human judgment, arbitrariness, and the essentially political—can come to the aid of morality but not of law. The essentially debatable threshold of the *intolerable* obliges us to fight with the arms of conscientious decision, not those of positive law.

The justification of international law is often based on texts from Renaissance thinkers, especially Hugo Grotius's famous work, *The Law of War and Peace* (1625).[2] In several important chapters, Grotius affirms that kings or other governments have the right to punish—even outside their borders—those who "excessively violate the natural law or the law of nations,"[3] including, for example, cannibals, pirates, and all those who act like wild beasts. As a positive example, Grotius invokes Hercules. He made it his task to deliver the earth of tyrants. Crossing the globe as a liberator, he was praised by the entirety of an admiring tradition.[4]

If, however, Grotius justified punishing foreign criminals who violate natural law and the law of nations more than they violate any positive law, he also understood by "punishment" *war*, in the cases mentioned above, waged in the name of justice. "War against them is natural," he writes of those who conduct themselves as wild beasts.[5] Or again: "Wars that are undertaken to punish are suspected of being unjust unless the crimes are very atrocious and very obvious."[6] In these ways, Grotius does propose, quite presciently, that punishing in the name of a law other than positive law is legitimate. This can involve violating other states' sovereignty. But this punishment takes the form of war, which means it mut be decided on a case-by-case basis. And he remains rather restrictive concerning the categories of tragic cases that call for it. We therefore can invoke Grotius today to legitimate just war, but justifying international law or justice is quite another matter.

One can endlessly debate at what point wars of humanitarian intervention are just. Our predecessors did so before us. In the sixteenth century, the *Vindiciae contra tyrannos* justified the right of intervention as "charity towards the persecuted," and Francisco Vitoria marked out its boundaries: "It is limited to the protection of the innocent and of Christians, and to the deposing of tyrants."[7]

With the rise of modern sovereignty, suspicion was raised concerning the right of intervention. "One cannot demand of a state that it renounce its constitution, even if it is despotic," wrote Kant (in *Perpetual Peace*).[8] And with his customary irony, Benjamin Constant said: "During the French Revolution people invented a heretofore unknown pretext for war, that of delivering peoples from the yoke of their governments held to be illegitimate and tyrannical. With this pretext one brought death to men, some of whom lived peacefully under institutions softened by time and custom, while others had for several centuries enjoyed the benefits of liberty. This was an eternally shameful period, in which a treacherous government inscribed sacred words on its guilty banners, troubled the peace, violated independence, destroyed the property of its innocent neighbors, and added to the scandal of Europe by its mendacious claims of respect for the rights of man and zeal for humanity! 'The worst of conquerors,' said Machiavelli, 'is the hypocrite, as though he were forecasting our history.'"[9]

The main criticism one can level against wars of intervention derives from the very nature of politics. Politics names the *adversary*, not *evil itself.* These are two very different things. Politics must designate and combat the adversary as one who injures, or risks injuring, the society one has the duty of protecting. In this way, "adversary" is a political category, while "evil" is a moral one. Politics attacks evil if it injures society. This is not the case with a war of intervention. If a true war of intervention exists, one conducted (to take a modern example) to liberate a people from its tyrant without any ulterior motive (such as oil), then it is conducted against evil and it is a moral war. It is as if politics had decided that the evil in question—this tyranny—represented an adversary of all humanity. In this context, politics transcends its normal role because it employs its powers to accomplish a moral task. Such a war is and will always remain debatable, which does not mean that it should never be undertaken, but that we are dealing here with matters of conscience and decision.

Opinions on the right of intervention naturally evolve with the times, espousing the dominant values of the period. Speaking generally, the opposite of what each period finds most important will not be tolerated. When religion dominated, it justified wars, as Montesquieu observed: "Religion gives to those who profess it a right to enslave those who do not, in order to more easily propagate it."[10] Today, one can say the same thing of the morality of human rights, while religion is compelled to be tolerant because it has assumed a lesser importance. Our grand declarations concerning tolerance often mask the truth and smack of hypocrisy, because each epoch demands freedom of thought in the domains it relativizes, while it is ready to defend with might-and-main what it holds to be absolute. Today, this means human rights in their contemporary version.

Carl Schmitt observed that the Westphalian formula *cuius regio eius religio* ("whose rule it is, is his religion"), which today we find so inconceivable, in fact earlier was first transformed into *cuius regio eius natio* ("his nation"), or into *cuius regio eius oeconomnia* ("his economic system"), depending upon what each epoch held to be essential.[11] Myriam Revault d'Allonnes has demonstrated that the idea of just war, which "in its essence is a missionary war or a crusade," was first justified by Christianity, then by the philosophies of history during the revolutionary era.[12] It is now justified by human rights. Obviously, war in the name of human rights today appears to us to be as justified as the crusades did to Christians in earlier times.

This last observation ought not to stop us from believing in absolute values, nor from wanting to defend them with all the means at our disposal, including force when other means fail. What it means is that a true appreciation of the legitimacy of a war of intervention sees it as a situated decision, bound to a time, a place, and to particular agents, none of which can be accounted for by a general or universal theory.

Such a decision simultaneously contains and expresses an internal certainty concerning good and evil and an awareness of uncertainty concerning their boundaries. In other words, this particular certainty cannot erect itself as a universal norm.

A decision concerning the legitimacy of a war of intervention must derive from a discernment by particular agents involved in a particular situation. As is always the case in a limit-situation, the decision has to be made in the depths of conscience; it must fully engage a person's being.

To use the contemporary idiom, the war of *humanitarian intervention* is a moral war, since the enemy is a criminal and not a political enemy in the sense of an adversary who assaults a particular people. Such a war is not conducted for the defense of a society or culture but rather is waged in the name of universal morality—or what is held to be universal. Nonetheless, the decision to engage in this kind of moral war is a *political* act, because it must be made by a particular political agent or society acting in the name of an injured other, in the way an individual comes to the aid of a neighbor. As soon as such a war is seen as a political act, there is no contradiction in taking on one tyrant rather than another, in attacking one rogue state while others remain unpunished. The universality demanded by law or pure justice is not required of a political decision. Conversely, if we decide to employ force to liberate a people or to stop monstrous governments from acting, we cannot cover ourselves with the blessing of the law. The particular character of *this* situation and *this* decision prevents us from transforming war into a legal police action.

Because a war of humanitarian intervention is an act of morality, it demands that we engage ourselves entirely. And this engagement first of all is physical. The intervention of Westerners in Serbia, even though it never received the blessing of international law, was always considered as the legal pursuit of an outlaw, as a police action, but *one in which the police did not expose themselves to harm* and shed none of their own blood. On the other hand, the American intervention in Iraq was a humanitarian war, undertaken in conscience and with the various risks assumed, including the loss of American lives. This corroborates Augustin Cochin's remark: "When one sheds others' blood, one does not have the right to spare one's own."[13] The Americans were no longer policemen redressing offenses within the confines of a legal system. They were outsiders who inserted themselves at their own peril in a battle that they considered justified. One of course can contest that judgment. But it is this possible contestation that implies the decision's genuinely human character.

CONCLUSION

FROM THE TIME the idea of world government began to dawn, the time of the Enlightenment, Kant saw the way in which this idea was self-destructive. His analysis is all the more relevant in that he himself was a man of the Enlightenment, and at the beginning of his reflections on this matter he had hoped for the advent of the *Weltstaat*.

The establishment of a world government would not, it was thought, be merely a quantitative step taken by humanity in order better to establish transnational or international justice. It would be a qualitative step, in the sense that a world government would clearly be of another nature than any other state, whether a federal or even an imperial one. By definition encompassing all earthly societies, it would have to be despotic, because all diversity—the condition for the continued existence of politics as we understand it—would be extinguished. The democratic state cannot exist except in the tensions of internal and external *multiplicity* and *competition*: that is, in a world open to the four winds. The world state closes the world by enclosing it in a single Thought, a single Idea of justice and the good. Assigning itself the task of realizing the moral universal, it must command and compel virtue and thereby destroy it, because there is no virtue without freedom. According to Kant, we can *aspire* to a universal republic, but we can only *realize* a universal despotism. And since world government is the necessary, even indispensable, corollary of an international justice worthy of the title "justice," if world government is undesirable because of its despotic character, so too is international justice.

Viewed from the perspective of our own time, the ideas of world government and international justice run into the same contradiction that shook, then toppled, the socialist ideal and regimes in the twentieth century. The socialist ideal envisaged the realization of a more just world by means of the consent of all. But in the face of the diversity of points of view it finally was realizable only by coercion, which destroyed its very essence. Socialism was abandoned because it required a continual recourse to coercion and terror, for which, finally, men did not have the stomach. In the same way, the idea of world government hesitates before the evidence of its despotic character. In order to be realized, both efforts must assault liberty, the necessary condition of morality.

We find ourselves before one of the common utopian ideas of European history. Our forebears from Plato to Marx believed in the establishment of an all-powerful and all-good power, one justified by the best principles. However, we are "of a time that has had many illusions shattered"; we have become capable of seeing through various mystifications.[1] We know by bitter experience that any power created and exercised by men is ipso facto incapable of that perfection indispensable for the just exercise of any monopoly. The perfect government, like the perfect man, does not exist. On the contrary, the more that a power is absolute and monopolistic, the more it will have the tendency to abuse its power. We no longer have the excuse of ignorance to think that because it embodies the highest morality a world government will produce the miraculous synthesis of total power and good government.

I think that we have to agree with the argument, which runs from Kant to Arendt, that the call for a world government represents a form of angelicism, which is always ripe to engender terror. Hannah

Arendt showed how our contemporaries, terrified by the crimes of states capable of wiping humanity off of the map, entertain "the hope that humanity will return to reason and that it will do away with politics rather than itself; that thanks to a world government which will absorb the state and make it an administrative instrument, political conflicts will be handled as bureaucratic matters, and armies will be replaced by police forces." She continues: "But this hope is completely utopian. . . . [W]e will end up with an even more monstrous form of despotic government."[2] And she adds a bit further on: this ideal, the socialist ideal, "is not at all utopian: it is simply horrifying." Put another way: if it is realized, the world government will become the gravedigger of man's humanity, "the state containing Nietzsche's last man," as Leo Strauss put it, that condition in which what is human in man cannot be satisfied.[3]

The attempt at world government and international justice simply demonstrates that this type of dangerous angelicism has not disappeared from our thinking, despite recent experiences. One may wonder whether this angelicism does not arise from the illusion that we entertain concerning the absolute, metaphysical character of the evil at work in the Holocaust. An international justice and by extension a world government that have as their goal the struggle against all forms of metaphysical evil and their offshoots could not but be absolutely good. Or so we think. We need to return to earth once more, where neither evil nor good exist in pure, disincarnate states.

The current organization of international justice presents itself as a "struggle against the forces of evil," and its adherents claim "to intervene in a pathology."[4] Everything is considered as if it were a question of eradicating evil from the earth. To want to judge everyone who did not disobey the laws of the state when necessary—in other words, to punish people for not being Antigone—is to judge in a perfectionist vein, which is clearly to act in an inquisitorial manner. Furthermore, the Treaty of Rome classifies as war crimes actions that can never be eradicated without the advent of a world totally without violence.

The paradox of international justice is also expressed in the spirit that animates it when it appears in public: it pursues its pedagogy moved by indignation. This is the way it tries to move public opinion. Justice, however, is not "educational"—it is not in the business of educating. Our "international justice" attempts to call citizens to the correct path and to teach them the good. But it does so by departing from democratic procedures. By identifying morality and the law, it takes on a theocratic form.

In truth, the "educative work" to which advocates of international justice devote themselves clearly indicates the incoherence of this type of justice in the human world. Truth be told, every utopia falls into fatal contradictions. In this case, we are given largely symbolic declarations: "Never again!" These are credible only on the condition that the world citizen who utters them can also identify with the guilty party. But that cannot be done, for in the same breath he declares that the guilty are moral monsters. And detached from their contexts, their situations, and their histories, they do appear to be devils come to earth rather than mere mortals. Far from committing all-too-human crimes, they are held to bring such evil into the world that the observer is convinced that he has nothing in common with such men.[5] In these circumstances, it is impossible to understand what the educative value of justice could be, and the "duty to remember" becomes a hollow phrase. The advocates of international justice have not understood that they cannot simultaneously isolate metaphysical evil and hold it up to all the world as a sort of negative model.

Besides their utopian-despotic character, the ideas of international justice and world government become properly relativized when one considers their history. They represent a hope that has already been tried—one that appeared in a certain context, even if it cannot simply be reduced to that context.

Arnold Toynbee provided an introduction to the point of view shared—not originated—by our contemporaries. In his *A Study of History*, Toynbee wrote several chapters on the universal states. Among them, he placed first of all the Roman empire, then those Western empires which were the heirs of Rome, whether the Holy Roman Empire or Peter the Great's. Finally, he lists the different Muslim and Asiatic empires.

The very fact that these other civilizations wrongly claimed universality should chasten *our* universalistic certitudes. By wanting—out of profound conviction, to be sure—to impose human rights on the entire globe, we reproduce an already well-known model, although the context and values have changed. Each one of these empires believed itself to be the sole or last universal empire, the unique possessor of truth and the good, according to which humanity's destiny would be finally realized. Others before us have believed that they were living at "the end of history." This rather common mistake calls into question the right we have to coerce others, even if it does not necessarily undermine our faith in and attachment to these values.

According to Toynbee, every "end of history" is characterized by a pacified state, an immobile or unchanging situation, and the sentiment that all wars and even all conflicts have disappeared for good. Towards the exterior, movement toward unification accelerates. By its mere presence, the universal empire annihilates every separate will-to-power that could contest it. It puts in place an uninterrupted process of cultural homogenization, a process of which it is the exemplar and engine. The movement within is toward centralization because intermediary authorities are undermined and the central government believes itself to be the sole competent judge. In this way, a universal peace is organized, one that encompasses once-rival peoples and different groups within each people. The concord is informed by a spirit and climate of nonviolence extended to all of society's domains. Conflicts and quarrels are replaced by holidays and the pleasures of daily life.

Given that Toynbee was the author of the famous phrase "challenge and response," one can well imagine that this situation did not seem to him to be a desirable one. It is obvious that the lasting peace thus obtained only comes about *after* the deep and revealing conflicts of human history. "The universal state seduces souls and hearts because it symbolizes salvation after the endless misery of a time of troubles."[6] To be sure, one cannot reproach men for preferring peace to war. However, this situation reveals an attempt to leave history rather than history's actual end. It is an illusion rather than salvation. Ultimately, it is a sign of impotence rather than wisdom.

For Toynbee, the desire for universality appears at times of decline. An exhausted civilization seeks to safeguard its future by affirming its immortality. (The desire for universality necessarily leads to the desire for immortality, as spatial infinity has to be connected to temporal infinity.) It is as if only a quasi-metaphysical guarantee could compensate for the inability to survive by normal human and historical means. Peoples who formerly were creative lose their vital energies. They find themselves unable to fight to defend their distinctive point of view and their very existence. No longer knowing how to vanquish their foes by force (whether of arms or argument), they "minimize" them by the seductive but fallacious idea of peace and repose without end. Thus, the desire for universality corresponds to the exhaustion of aged peoples.

One could retort that this senility, which as such is regrettable, perhaps can give rise to happiness by other routes. This view, however, is not Toynbee's. For him, real rivalry is a powerful stimulus that alone allows for progress in history, for reform and improvement. The peace of the universal state expresses "a process of psychological disarmament," which is why these empires will always be overcome by younger, less "civilized" peoples who lack this idealism of perpetual peace.[7]

Everything indicates that the maintenance of true diversity—an admittedly demanding task—remains in the hands of young energetic cultures that are confident in themselves. On the other hand, when a culture shows itself to be tired of conflicts, and even of mere disputes, pursuing the universal seems to represent its sole chance of survival.

Everyone knows that international justice was first proposed by Americans, and that it was initially criticized by Europeans. Contemporary Europeans' desire to replace war with justice is a response to a changed historical situation. It is very likely that it will collapse, like so many other angelicisms, before the unalterable *mediocrity* of the human condition. Wise minds know that the human condition always has the last word. The demands, even the expectations, for international justice and world government are essentially poisonous flowers sprouting among rather fortunate peoples who naïvely believe themselves to be all-powerful and who have lost the idea and the sense of the tragic in life. These periods of good fortune do not last. Reality always catches the stragglers who think they have outrun and overcome it.

However, no false idea is wholly disconnected from reality. The demand for international justice and world government bears (and conceals) the legitimate hope of humanity to advance, step by step, to unity, much as the Little Prince did on his way to the fountain. But this means that the contemporary desire for total justice is doomed not only to failure, but it inhibits the only search for justice that can succeed. The proposed (and pretended) conquest inhibits the reasonable quest. Western arrogance engenders and increases opposition to the West. Justice is done but at the cost of growing animosity: Milosevic and Seseli, both incarcerated in the international prison at Scheveninger, won elections in Serbia. . . .

It is only when we realize these things that we will be able to begin the patient work of persuasion, to provide examples that will improve the world. As Las Casas said, there is only one way to evangelize the world, and it most certainly is not by force.

NOTES

INTRODUCTION

1. *Mémoire du mal, tentation du bien*, Robert Laffont, 2000, 302.
2. "Du droit des peoples au droit des citoyens du monde?", *Le Monde des débats*, n. 1, November 1999, 7.
3. "Progrès et limites de la moralization de l'organisation internationale", in *Morale et relations internationales*, PUF, 2000, 63.
4. *Les Grands Procès politiques*, E. Le Roy Ladurie, Ed., du Rocher, 2002, 194.

CHAPTER 1

1. *La République universelle ou Adresse aux tyrannicides*, Oeuvres, Munich, 1980, v. III, 344–45.
2. *Bases constitutionnelles de la République du genre humain*, ibid., 620.
3. A. Kojève in Leo Strauss, *De la tyrannie*, Gallimard, 1954, 233.
4. John Fonte, "Liberal Democracy v. Transnational Progressivism," Hudson Center, October 26, 2001.
5. P. A. Taguieff, "L'emprise du néoprogressisme", *Le Figaro*, July 2, 2003.

6. Garry Davis was a pilot in the United States Air Force. In May 1948, he tore up his American passport in front of the U.S. Embassy in Paris. On November 19, 1948, he appeared before the assembly of the United Nations to call for the creation of a world government. A number of intellectuals of the time, including Albert Camus, André Gide, and Jean-Paul Sartre, admired and defended him.

7. See for example, J. Maritain, *L'Homme et l'État*, Oeuvres complètes, v. IX, Éd. universitaires de Fribourg, 1990.

CHAPTER 2

1. *The Idea of a Universal History from a Cosmopolitan Point of View*, 8th proposition.
2. Ibid., 5th proposition.
3. Ibid., 5th & 7th propositions.
4. VIII, 311.
5. Idem.
6. *Pour la paix perpétuelle*, Presses universitaires de Lyon, 1985, 64.
7. Ibid., 87–88.
8. Ibid., 89
9. *La Paix perpétuelle. Le bicentenaire d'une idée kantienne*, Le Cerf.
10. Ibid., 74.
11. Ibid, 49.
12. Ibid., 77–80.
13. Ibid., 89.
14. "Perpetual Peace," in *Perpetual Peace and Other Essays,* trans. Ted Humphrey (Indianapolis, IN: Hackett Publishing Company, 1983), 123.
15. Ibid., 139.

CHAPTER 3

1. *La Différence entre les systèmes philosophiques de Fichte et de Schelling*, trans. B. Gilson, Vrin, 1986, p 161–62.
2. *Fiat justitia, pereat Germania!*, in *Écrits politiques*, Champ libre, 1977, 40ff.
3. Crimes internationaux et jurisdictions internationals, PUF, 2000, 18.
4. *Crimes internationaux*, 71.

CHAPTER 4

1. *The Spirit of the Laws*, XXVI, 2.
2. Ibid., I, 3.
3. Ibid., XV, 7 & 8.
4. Ibid., XIX, 20.
5. *Defense of the Spirit of the Laws*, 2nd part.
6. Ibid., XIX, 14.
7. Ibid., XIX, 27.
8. *Observation sur le 29th livre de l'Esprit des lois, Oeuvres completes*, Didot, 1847, v. 1, ch. XVIII.
9. Ibid.
10. *Bases constitutionnelles de la République du genre humain*, 621.
11. Ibid., 633. "Level the Republic without any exceptions, subordinate men to things, functionaries to their function, individuals to the mass, society to law"; ibid., 635; or: "I propose an absolute leveling, a total overturning of all the barriers that thwart the interests of the human family," *La République universelle ou Adresse aux tyrannices*, v. III, 347.
12. *Bases constitutionnelles*, 632.
13. *Mémoire du mal, tentation du bien*, 293–96.
14. Ibid., 302.

CHAPTER 5

1. *Eichmann à Jerusalem*, Gallimard, 1997, 340–41.
2. *Des crimes qu'on ne peut ni punir ni pardoner*, Odile Jacob, 2002, 168; or 174: "How can one imagine that the accused is not guilty and therefore already half-condemned?"
3. Axel Poullard, *Regard ethnographique sur le TPI pour l'ex-Yougoslavie*, private document, 44–45.
4. Morale et relations internationals, IRIS, Paris, 2000, 141f.
5. Summit of the G-7, cf. Pascal Boniface, *Morale et relations internationales*, PUF, 2000, 12.
6. *Crimes internationaux*, Claude Jorda, 72.

7. XV, 7 & 8.

8. XV, 7.

9. Bernal Diaz del Castillo, *Histoire véridique de la conquete de la Nouvelle-Espagne*, La Découverte, 2003, v. I, 213.

10. Michael Oakeshott, "Rationalism in Politics," from *Rationalism in Politics and Other Essays*, foreword by Timothy Fuller (Indianapolis, IN: Liberty Fund, 1991), 31.

11. Ibid. 32–33.

12. Jacques Dewitte, "Études phénoménologiques," *Ousia*, 1996, n. 23–24, "La redécouverte de la question téléologique," 14ff.

13. *Essais*, Gallimard, 1965. I develop these points in a previous work, *The Unlearned Lessons of the Twentieth Century* (ISI Books, 2006).

CHAPTER 6

1. "La criminalization du monde," in *Le Droit penal à l'épreuve de l'internationalisation*, Bruylant, 2002, 337ff; or Antoine Garapon, *Des crimes*, 190: "The thousand of genocides in the prisons of Kigali most often do not think themselves guilty."

2. *Qu'est-ce que les Lumières?* Hatier, 1999, 41.

3. For example, Ronny Abraham, "Le droit international peut-il régir le monde?," in *Morale et relations internationales*, PUF, 2000, 51.

4. Cf. John Rosenthal, "Les ambiguities de la CPI," *Le Figaro*, July 16, 2002.

5. Crimes internationaux, 65.

6. *Esquisse*, "Tenth epoch".

7. *Nous et les autres*, Le Seuil, 1989, 50ff.

CHAPTER 7

1. Cf. Anne-Marie Pelletier, *Lectures bibliques*, Le Cerf, 1973, 65ff.

2. *Un nuage comme un tapis*, Payot-Rivages, 1996, "Le don des langues," 20.

3. Chapters XII & XIII.

4. Chapter XIII

5. Ibid.

6. *The Spirit of the Laws*, chapter XIX, 18: "There are certain ideas of uniformity that

sometimes seize hold of great minds but which infallible diminish smaller ones. They find in them a kind of perfection. . . ."

7. *L'État universel*, Gallimard, 1990, 71.

8. Ibid., 40.

9. Ibid., 62.

10. Jean Bodin published *The Six Books of the Republic* in 1576, four years after the Saint Bartholomew Day massacre; Hobbes published the *Leviathan* in 1651, in the aftermath of the English Civil War.

CHAPTER 8

1. François Guizot, *Histoire de la civilization en Europe*, Didier, 1846, 2nd lesson, 37.

2. *Le Regard mutilé, schizophrénie culturelle, pays traditionnels face à la modernité*, L'Aube Poche, 1996, 46–47.

3. *Culture et droits de l'homme*, Hachette, 1992, 116.

4. *La Guerre et la Paix*, Tops/Trincquier, 1998, v. I, 41.

5. *The Idea of a Universal History from a Cosmopolitan Point of View*, 4th proposition.

6. *La Vie de l'esprit*, 1, 34.

7. *Perpetual Peace*, 1st addition.

CHAPTER 9

1. "As if polygamy could coexist with national liberty!", *La République universelle*, 351.

2. *Bases constitutionnelles*, 614.

3. *Structures*, La Table Ronde, 2003, 257.

4. Sophie Bessis and Driss el Yazami, *Le Monde*, October 24, 2002.

5. *Le Monde*, November 11, 2002.

6. Ibid.

CHAPTER 10

1. *Les Deux Sources de la morale et de la religion*, PUF, 2000, 284.

2. *Non-lieux, introduction à une anthropologie de la surmodernité*, Le Seuil, 1992.

3. *Actuelles* I, "Je réponds," et "Réponse à l'incrédule".

4. *Penser l'Europe à ses frontières*, L'Aube, 1993, 51.

5. *Non-lieux*

6. This justice is called "groundless". Cf. P. Hazan and C. N. Robert, "La criminalisation du monde," in *Le Droit pénal à l'épreuve de l'internationalisation,* 337.

CHAPTER 11

1. Sophocles, *Antigone*, II, 1.

2. This is the most probable interpretation. It is possible that the divisions are more complex. Stamatios Tzitia shows that at a time when the positive laws were not yet written, Antigone contrasts the customary law to the arbitrary law of the prince. "Scolies sur les *nomina* d'Antigone représentées comme droit naturel," *Archives de philosophie du droit*, 1988, 243–59.

3. *Mémoire du mal*, 288.

4. *Cultures et droits de l'homme,* 80ff.

5. Ibid., 103.

6. Cf. Antonio Cassese, *Crimes internationaux et jurisdictions internationales,* 20: "We have a kind of new natural law (*droit*), but one that belongs to positive law: these are the imperative norms of international law, which ratify the fundamental values with which all states ought to comply."

7. Michel Villey, *La Formation de la pensée juridique moderne*, Montchrestien, 1975, 362.

8. Idem.

9. Pierre Mesnard, *L'Essor de la philosophie politique au XVI siècle,* 656.

10. *Réflexions sur la justice*, Plon, 2001, 258.

11. Cf. Barbara Koehn, *La Résistance allemande contre Hitler*, PUF, 2003.

12. *Eichmann à Jerusalem,* 471.

CHAPTER 12

1. *La Paix perpétuelle,* 57.

2. *Pouvoir et contre-pouvoir à l'ère de la mondialisation*, Aubier, 2002, 551–52.

CHAPTER 13

1. *Ni victims ni bourreaux,* 328ff.

2. Dom Robert Le Gall and Lama Jigmé Rinpoché, *Le Moine et le lama*, Fayard, 2001, 191.

3. *L'Essence de politique*, Sirey, 1965, 487.

4. Cf. Bergson, *Les Deux Sources de la morale et de la religion,* 25–35; 284–85; and Jacques Maritain, *L'Homme et l'État*, 726–27, 732.

5. *Pensées diverses*, Montesquieu's self-portrait.

6. *Traité de la nature humaine*, Aubier, 1946, II, section IV, 455.

7. P. Mesnard, 654.

8. Cf. B. Bourgeois, *La Raison moderne et le droit politique*, Vrin, 2000, 196ff.

9. Cf. A. Wellmer, *Libéraux et communautariens*, PUF, 1997, 397–99.

CHAPTER 14

1. *La Quête du Graal*, Le Seuil, 1965, 163.

CHAPTER 15

1. *Actuelles* I, "Ni victims ni bourreaux," 347.

2. Ibid., 349.

3. *The Spirit of the Laws*, XIX, 14.

4. Ibid., XIX, 8.

5. *La Pesanteur et la grâce*, Plon, 1988, 72.

6. *Les Deux Sources* , 74.

7. Ibid., 97.

8. Ibid., 74–75.

CHAPTER 16

1. *Verbum Caro*, v. I, n. 3.

2. *Le Droit de la guerre et de la paix*, PUF, 1999, II, ch. 20, paragraph 11, 1.

3. Ibid., 3.

4. Ibid., 2.

5. Ibid., 3.

6. Ibid., paragraph xliii, 3.

7. Cf. Pierre Mesnard, 346; p. 464. See also Stephen Launay, *La Guerre sans la guerre*, Descartes et Cie, 2003.

8. Op. cit., 77–78.

9. *De l'esprit de conquête* . . . , ch. viii, 105.

10. *The Spirit of the Laws*, XV, 4.

11. *La Notion de politique*, Calmann-Lévy, 1972, 143.

12. *Fragile humanité. L'idée de guerre juste a-t-elle encore un sens?*, Aubier, 2002, 121.

13. *L'Esprit du jacobinisme*, 189.

CONCLUSION

1. E. Cioran, Essay sur la pensee reactionnaire, Fata Morgana, 1977, 10.

2. *Qu'est-ce que la politique?* Le Seuil, 1995, 46–47.

3. *De la tyrannie*, 337.

4. Cf. N. Robert, in *Le Droit penal à l'épreuve de l'internationalisation*, 339.

5. Cf. T. Todorov, "Les limites de la justice," in *Crimes internationaux*, 42–44.

6. *L'Histoire*, Elsevier-Sequoia, 1978, 389.

7. Ibid., 401

INDEX

ABOUT THE AUTHOR AND TRANSLATOR

CHANTAL DELSOL is a professor of philosophy at the University of Marne-La-Vallée near Paris. Recently elected to the prestigious Académie des Sciences Morales et Politiques (Institut de France), she is also a novelist. Her other titles in English are the critically hailed *Icarus Fallen: The Search for Meaning in an Uncertain World* and *The Unlearned Lessons of the Twentieth Century: An Essay on Late Modernity*, both published by ISI Books.

PAUL SEATON, assistant professor of philosophy at St. Mary's Seminary and University in Baltimore, is the translator of several books and articles by prominent French thinkers, including Pierre Manent's *Democracy without Nations? The Fate of Self-Government in Europe*, which is also included in ISI Books' Crosscurrents series. He is currently writing a book on the thought of Pierre Manent.